T0078131

CRACKING *the* GENTLEMAN'S CODE

A GUIDE TO
Becoming the Job 29 Man

KGOMOTSO MAMELLO MOTSHIDI

WESTBOW
PRESS®
A DIVISION OF THOMAS NELSON
& ZONDERVAN

The Holy Bible, English Standard Version® (ESV®)
Copyright © 2001 by Crossway,
a publishing ministry of Good News Publishers.
All rights reserved.
ESV Text Edition: 2016

Scripture taken from the King James Version of the Bible.

Scripture quotations marked MSG are taken from THE MESSAGE, copyright © 1993, 1994, 1995, 1996, 2000, 2001, 2002 by Eugene H. Peterson. Used by permission of NavPress. All rights reserved. Represented by Tyndale House Publishers, Inc.

Scripture quotations marked (NIV) are taken from the Holy Bible, New International Version®, NIV®. Copyright © 1973, 1978, 1984, 2011 by Biblica, Inc.™ Used by permission of Zondervan. All rights reserved worldwide. www.zondervan.com The "NIV" and "New International Version" are trademarks registered in the United States Patent and Trademark Office by Biblica, Inc.™

This book is a work of non-fiction. Unless otherwise noted, the author and the publisher make no explicit guarantees as to the accuracy of the information contained in this book and in some cases, names of people and places have been altered to protect their privacy.

WestBow Press books may be ordered through booksellers or by contacting:

WestBow Press
A Division of Thomas Nelson & Zondervan
1663 Liberty Drive
Bloomington, IN 47403
www.westbowpress.com
1 (866) 928-1240

Because of the dynamic nature of the Internet, any web addresses or links contained in this book may have changed since publication and may no longer be valid. The views expressed in this work are solely those of the author and do not necessarily reflect the views of the publisher, and the publisher hereby disclaims any responsibility for them.

Any people depicted in stock imagery provided by Thinkstock are models, and such images are being used for illustrative purposes only. Certain stock imagery © Thinkstock.

ISBN: 978-1-9736-1114-1 (sc)
ISBN: 978-1-9736-1115-8 (e)

Print information available on the last page.

WestBow Press rev. date: 12/20/2017

To the memory of our beloved brother,
Katlego Motshidi.

Contents

Foreword...xi

Acknowledgements... xiii

Introduction..xv

Chapter 1   The Quest to Seek.. 1

Chapter 2   Breaking the Altars of the Fathers............. 21

Chapter 3   Living Sacrifices 45

Chapter 4   Behind the Suit..65

Chapter 5   For such a time as this.................................87

Chapter 6   Becoming the Job 29 Man......................... 107

Dedication

First and foremost, I dedicate this book to the King eternal, immortal, invisible, the only wise God our Saviour unto Him be glory and majesty, dominion and power, both now and ever.

To the memory of Katlego Motshidi…In his own words *'If God gave me a choice to choose another family to do life with, I'd choose you guys again.'* We thank God for the gift you were to us.

To my parents, Ishmael and Mpho Motshidi, thank you for loving us and being there for us. Thank you for raising us in the knowledge and fear of God.

To Bishop Mosa and Pastor Gege Sono thank you for leading with integrity and for loving God and His people. Thank you for the teachings that have transformed our lives.

To all the men and women of God who planted the seed of faith in my life and nurtured me, thank you.

Foreword

As the chronicles of history are written, it will be recorded that Kgomotso and Katlego are the best older siblings anyone could ever ask for. After Katli's (Katlego) passing Kgomi (Kgomotso) decided she wanted to write a book in his honour, and it came as no surprise. Initially one would have imagined that it would be styled as a biography, however, writing about the intrinsic characteristics that defined the man we closely knew as brother, was befitting.

In one of the last forms of communication we had, Katli wrote "…only God can change a man" Those words couldn't be any truer. Katli was the embodiment of a true gentle(man) – inside and out. Much more than the slim-fit suits, barbered hair and goatee; his smile, generosity, loving, humorous, kind and gentle demeanor transcended boundaries, making him easy to love and relate to. Not only did he know God's Word, but it was his daily quest to live by it. Psalms 119:9 asks the question: "How can a young man correct his way?" The answer: "by obeying Your words". He did just that. In so doing, it can be said that he did crack the code.

For some time, much has been written *about* men, but seldom *to* men. That is the difference with this book. Through the pages of this book much introspection shall be done. The content is thought-provoking, hard-hitting and compels one to get in the Word of God in order to start living life by God's design – becoming the man God intends one to be. In her writing, Kgomi has done well in journeying with the reader – journeying into thoughts, actions and mindsets such that at the end of it all, transformation of the whole being occurs. This body of work will outlive its writer, and more importantly, generations of men the world over will be transformed and impacted by God's Word through this timeless body of work.

Kamogelo Motshidi

Acknowledgements

I would like to express my heartfelt gratitude to Kamogelo, my sister, who allowed me to bounce ideas off her as I was writing the manuscript. I would also like to thank Pastor Karabo Selepe, Pastor Musa Khanyile, Brian Mabe, Nduduzo Phili, Sibani Mngomezulu, Sibusiso Dube as well as Richard Masethe, who read the manuscript and gave me their candid feedback. To the WestBow Press team, thank you for believing in this vision with me.

Introduction

WE FARE THEE W(H)ELL

I write this book as a tribute to my brother, Katlego Motshidi, affectionately known as 'Katli'. He was killed in a fatal car crash, a head on collision that claimed his life and that of a relative, Isaac 'Ike' Mahlomola Motsamai, my cousin Kerileng's husband. It was on the evening of 05 February 2016 that we jovially gathered to celebrate the achievement of Ike and Kerileng's daughter Mpho, who was leaving home to resume her studies at University. The atmosphere was lively and jubilant as decorations and balloons sprawled around the house, with a particularly glittery banner with the words 'Bye-Bye Mpho' greeted each person at the entrance. What started as a small family gathering soon became a full house of people eager to congratulate the matriculant and bid her farewell on a new journey far from home. Ike and Katli, being the gentlemen they were, took it upon themselves to go out to the nearby stores to augment the snacks to ensure those celebrating with us were well catered for. As the evening progressed, Ike and Katli delayed to return. We were ready to hear Ike's speech as the organiser of the send-off, and of course as father to the celebrant. As their arrival from the stores tarried, those of us gathered…and hungry, said a short prayer and the festivities continued.

Shortly into the night, what started as an evening of celebration soon started playing out like scenes from a bad, tragic movie. The emergency services managed to contact us, informing us that there has been a fatal accident, involving Katlego and Ike. Unfortunately, Ike passed on and Katlego was airlifted to hospital and he was in a critical condition.

And so it was… two astute men of our family were involved in something so tragic and heart-breaking. We did not know how all this would end. How could an evening meant for celebration be marred by such an atrocity? I had to call my parents to inform them of what had happened.

Me: "*Ma, there has been an accident involving Ike and Katli. Ike has passed on and Katli is airlifted to hospital!*"

Mom: "*Oh my goodness! You stay there and comfort your sister (Ike's wife), Papa and I will go and see Katli…he will be okay.*"

Me: "*Okay mom just keep praying!*"

The emergency services kept updating us about Katli's condition. He had lost a lot of blood and was critical. We contacted an Aunt of ours, Winnie Kodisang, to intercept the helicopter and for her to update us on the situation until my parents arrived at the local hospital. My aunt kept updating us at intermittent intervals. Every time I picked up the phone, it was with baited breath as each call ignited hope that there will be good news on the other end of the line, and that he would make it. We spread the message to our prayer networks and church community that they intercede for us. We believed he would make it. In the early hours of 06 February 2016, another update call came, this time from Winnie's daughter, Phina.

Phina: "*Kgomi, Howzit[1]?*"

Me: "*I am fine, under the circumstances, Mama Winnie has been updating me, last I heard he is going into theatre... he lost a lot of blood...*"

She listened attentively and was very calm.

Phina: "*Kgomi, I don't know how to break this to you,*" she said calmly "*...but Katli didn't make it...He's no more.... I am so sorry, so sorry Kgomi...*"

I froze. I now had to face an already wailing house, only to tell them that Katlego also didn't make it. This was a double tragedy. Every time I took a call, eyes were on me. I had to be calm as I broke the news that Katlego was also no more. My sister and cousins glared at me. I slowly gave them the update.

---

[1] Howzit, a greeting in South Africa, meaning How are you?

Me: "*I just received another update from the hospital... Unfortunately Katli didn't make it...*"

The wails became louder. The house that was decorated with balloons that earlier resembled a jovial mood turned into a house of pain, tears and confusion. We were a family broken and in pain. The reality of what we were facing kicked in. Days became weeks, which became months, a year and then some, having to adjust to the 'new normal'. Needless to say, through this tragedy and pain, we saw our family, friends and church community rally around us with support. Above all, God come through and He provided the healing. We saw facets of God like never before. We saw God the Comforter. We saw God the Healer. We saw God the Provider. We saw God the Restorer.

Thinking about the balloons that decorated the house, it was a farewell of a different kind. We were indirectly bidding them farewell. When Katlego would pronounce the word well, for some reason, he would have an emphatic 'h', and say "w(h)ell!" The thing is there is no 'h' in well! We would laugh about it and he would deliberately pronounce it that way...but I believe you can understand when through this book, we bid him *fare w(h)ell*!

THE GOD TIME SESSIONS

Katlego's life will not be defined by the moment he died, but by the memories and life we shared together. On the 05 February at 18:00, before leaving, the three of us as siblings had our last *God Time* session. Katlego led devotions and then reflected on his day as follows:

Katlego: "*Guys, tonight I feel different. For the first time in my life I feel totally surrendered to God. Today, I was meditating on the book of Job. Often when we think of Job making sacrifices, we think he made them mainly for God to build a hedge. I realised, he made them in order for him and his children not to curse God in their hearts...So guys, whatever happens, don't curse God.*"

We gave each other high-fives, my sister and I commented that we never saw it like that before, we prayed, got ready and left. In true Katli style, our last memorable moment shared together was *God Time*. He was a man who loved God and through the testimony of his life we know for him *to live is Christ and to die is gain* (Phil 1:20). At his funeral service my sister Kamogelo said: "Katli put *gentle* in *gentle*man!" The consistent testimony about his life was his infectious smile, humility, polite manners, his love for people and gentle demeanour. He left an indelible mark with everyone who came into contact with him.

Our relationship was entrenched growing up in Pimville, Soweto- ours was a tight siblingship! One day, while my brother was in his teens, we were walking home from a Cell Group meeting. A friend of ours, Nomonde Willem, encouraged us to spend our time together in devotions- she called it *'God Time'*. The idea was instead of just doing devotions as a duty, but rather to look at it as time with God. This perspective and that dedicated time with God changed our lives! We would allocate time from 9pm for the devotions, but beyond talking about God, we talked about everything! Our lives, our visions and how to make God an integral part of our life plans. *God Time* would sometimes end at 2:00 in the morning...it was that good! Through the *God Time* sessions my brother opened up his hopes, dreams, ambitions and fears. This allowed us to relate and develop an open and honest relationship where we were vulnerable to each other as siblings, but mostly vulnerable to God. Through the depth of our conversations he morphed from being just an ordinary guy to being the man who many grew to respect. He was loud in his quietness. An oxymoron of note...but somehow gentle as he was, humble as he was, there was depth in his being that made people around him to stop and recognise.

The thing he would say and mention often is that "*Only God can Change a Man.*" I ponder on that statement realising that throughout his life, he surrendered his body, soul and spirit to God. We grew up in Zone 6 Pimville, Soweto notoriously known as *Mgababa²*, some of the young men from our neighbourhood end up in jail and some perpetuate the negative stereotypes that label black men. I can only imagine the inner battles he had to fight as a Christian African Man. As a Christian first, the daily decisions to follow God's word unequivocally. Secondly, as an African, having to deal with being racially profiled. Thirdly as a man...guys you know that some things were only privy to the guys!

---

² Mgababa – a slang word to describe our section in the township

In the process of growth, he had to prune certain habits, friends and colleagues. He knew the man God called him to be and he intentionally invested in ensuring that he would guard his heart and actions in becoming the man God intended him to be. He lived by 2 Corinthians 4:7 which says *'But we have this treasure in jars of clay to show that all-surpassing power is from God and not from us' (NIV)*. This verse was his mantra. He worked hard to preserve the treasure that was revealed to him. He pursued purity, he sacrificially gave his time and resources, he served people with humility and with a consistent smile.

Katlego loved God and His people and this was evident in his level of servitude at our Church and Community. He served faithfully from his youth in our church and was also a mentor for young boys, at our *alma mater* Nkholi Primary School.

He studied his MBA at MIB School of Management in the quaint city of Trieste, Italy. For his funeral service, his roommate, Michael Premm, flew down to South Africa from Austria, to be with us as a family. Furthermore, on the weekend of 21-22 May 2016 a reunion was held in his honour at MIB School of Management by the Alumni Association and friends from around the world bore testimony of his gentle demeanour in and out the lecture room. An aunt of ours, Olga Maluleka, also flew in from the UK to be with us during the reunion. The church community he belonged to while in Italy, Tre Evangelica, were also there for us to provide support, it was evident that he meant a lot to those who were around him.

Through the pages of this book I will provide a glimpse into some of the *God Time* conversations that changed the trajectory of my brother's life. I remember us candidly talking about topics that I believe a lot of men would relate with. It is these topics that I believe you can reflect on as God works in you to change your life. I believe there is a remnant of men, who like my brother, by living according to God's statutes will be live out their purpose, change their families and even in the broader society and be regarded as *gentle*men!

'It is the glory of God to conceal a thing: but the honour of kings is to search out a matter'
Proverbs 25:2

1

The Quest to Seek

In the thirteenth century the Venetian explorer Marco Polo, went on expeditions in Asia to the Mongolian Empire. His expeditions entailed discovering the silk route and his journeys made him one of the greatest explorers of all time. His influence was so great, that the Kublai Khan, the Emperor at the time, expressed interest in Christianity and requested that he bring along a hundred missionaries[i]. Upon returning to Venice he recruited missionaries as per the Emperor's request and only two signed up[ii]. While on the journey back to Mongolia, the hardships of the journey made the recruits turn back. However, Marco Polo continued with the expedition and later served the Khan as his advisor. Had more missionaries signed up, can you imagine how far reaching the influence of Christianity could have been in the Mongolian Empire even up to modern day Asia. The missionaries had a great opportunity to influence a nation with the gospel and it was missed. Life is about seeking and seizing opportunities. Seeking is looking for something in a desperate manner. That which you seek becomes a point of focus.

Proverbs 25:2b says '...*the honour of kings is to search out a matter*'. Think about Simeon who was seeking the Lord waiting for the coming of the Messiah. He sought the Lord until Jesus was brought to the temple (Luke 2:22-35). When you determine that you will seek out a matter that is an encumbrance to your heart, then honour follows. You may have a burden to reach new frontiers in family, ministry, business, career, sports or even technology- don't let it go! Honour is granted when a matter is sought out. Marco Polo played his part, challenged himself, explored uncharted territories and history remembers him. Simeon sought the Lord until the Messiah was revealed to him. I believe there is a purpose for you being born as a man in your generation. For you to serve your generation and to receive honour you need to search out the matter. Search out the matter for your existence. Search out the matter for your purpose. Search out the matter for your life. Search out the matter for your family. Search out the matter for your race. Search out the matter and eventually your life will glorify God. Simply put, delve into God's word such that God can reveal the matter pertinent to you fulfilling your destiny.

When God created man the purpose was clear to be fruitful and multiply, have dominion and subdue the earth.

'And God said, Let us make man in our image, after our likeness: and let them have dominion...And God

blessed them, and God said unto them, Be fruitful, and multiply, and replenish the earth, and subdue it: and have dominion...' (Genesis 1:26,28)

The word man in this context refers to *homo sapiens* (human race), not just the male species. God made man in His image so that, His glory can be revealed. The Psalmist says: *'What is man that you are mindful of him...that you made him a little lower than God'* (Psalms 8:4-5). Man was made in God's image, the Hebrew translation for God in this context is Elohim- God majestic ruler over all things. Imagine that, God who is ruler over all things, the King eternal and immortal made you in His image. What an honour! God created you as a triune being, such that all of you, your spirit, soul and body bring honour to Him. In order to find and fulfil the purpose God has predestined for you, it is up to you to seek. Be like Marco Polo and Simeon, be on a mission to seek...The journey to seek starts with seeking first the Kingdom of God, then seeking the Lord and ultimately seeking His Word.

1. Seek First The Kingdom of God

> But **seek ye first the Kingdom of God**,
> *and his righteousness; and all these*
> *things shall be added unto you.*
> *(Matthew 6:33)*

Seeking the Kingdom of God should come first. This verse speaks of setting priorities in place. What is 'The Kingdom of God?' The Old and New Testament allude to the Kingdom of God. From the beginning all the way to the book of Revelations, there are images of magnificence referring to the King and His Kingdom. The pearly white gates, the streets of gold, Him seated on the throne…Oh, the splendour of His glory!

There are references made in the Old Testament about God and His Kingdom:

Psalms 93:2 (NIV)

'Your throne was established from long ago, you are from all eternity'

Isaiah 6:1

'…I saw the Lord, sitting on the throne, high and lifted up, and the train of His robe filled the temple'

Isaiah 9:7

'…Upon the throne of David and over His Kingdom, to order it and establish it with judgement and justice…'

Lamentations 5:19

'You, O Lord, remain forever; Your throne from generation to generation'

Similar New Testament references to the Kingdom of God:

Mark 1:15(ESV)

'*...The time is fulfilled, and the Kingdom of God is at hand...*'

Luke 22:30

'*That ye may eat and drink at my table in My Kingdom and sit on the thrones judging the twelve tribes of Israel*'

Acts 7:49

'*Heaven is my throne and earth is My footstool...*'

Hebrews 1:8

'*...Thy throne, O God, is for ever and ever: a sceptre of righteousness is a sceptre of Thy Kingdom*'

Revelation 4:3

'*...and there was a rainbow round about the throne, in sight like unto an emerald*'

Before we can understand the 'Kingdom of God', let us see how an earthly kingdom compares to God's Kingdom. There are parallels we can observe. We can say that the earthly kingdom is a pseudo of what God's Kingdom is.

We have Kings, The Kingdom, the Rules, Subjects and Security.

Kingdom Comparisons[iii]

	Earthly Kingdom	God's Kingdom
KING	The sovereign ruler, seat of authority	God reigns in sovereignty (Ps 45:6)
KINGDOM	The domain and territory of the kingdom	God rules over all (Ps 103:19)
RULES	Overarching protocols, procedures and regulations	God's judgements and ordinances are just and fair (Ps 89:14)
SUBJECTS	The citizens of the kingdom	We become part of God's kingdom by being born again(John 3:3)
SECURITY	The Army to keep law and order	God is the 'Commander in Chief of the Armies of Heaven', the Lord of Hosts – Jehovah Sibbaoath (Is 47:4))

God's Kingdom:

God reigns in sovereignty

Psalms 45:6 (NIV)

'Your throne, O God will last for ever and ever; a sceptre of justice will be the sceptre of your throne'

God rules over all.

Psalms 103:19

'The Lord hath prepared His throne in the heavens and His Kingdom ruleth overall'

He provided His statutes and ordinances for us to live by.

Psalms 89:14

'Justice and judgement are the habitation of thy throne: mercy and truth shall go before thy face'

We obtain Kingdom citizenry by being born gain, receiving the gift of His son Jesus.

John 3:3

'Verily, verily I say unto thee, except a man be born again, he cannot see the Kingdom of God'

We obtain protection as He commands the heavenly hosts.

Isaiah 47:4

'As for our redeemer, the Lord of Hosts is His name, the Holy One of Israel'

Jesus Himself makes reference to the Kingdom of God. He has several teachings and parables that make us see that there is a Kingdom of God.

'...The Kingdom of God is at hand' (Mark 1:15)

'...The Kingdom of God is within you' (Luke17:21)

'...Suffer the little children...for of such is the Kingdom of God' (Luke 18:16).

'But if I cast out devils by the Spirit of God, then the Kingdom of God is come unto you' (Matthew 12:28)

'...What shall we say the Kingdom of God is like...' (Mark 4:30) NIV

From the scriptures it is indicative that reference to the Kingdom of God can be dichotomised. The Kingdom is spiritual as well as physical. To ultimately see the physical Kingdom, it starts with seeking after things that are spiritual. Jesus *said: 'The Kingdom of God is within you'(Luke 17:21)*. Similarly, the Apostle Paul in Romans 14:17 says: *'The Kingdom of God is not meat and drink, but righteousness, and peace and joy in the Holy Ghost'.* Both scriptures refer to the Kingdom of God being a manifestation of intangible attributes (spiritual). Jesus speaks of the Kingdom of God within you. That which is within you cannot be seen with the natural eye, it is intangible. When Paul refers to the Kingdom of God, he first negates things we see in this physical realm- that is meat and drink, he then goes on to say what the Kingdom of God *is*. He starts with righteousness- right standing with God. He then refers to peace- the peace of God that passes understanding. He lastly refers to joy- the joy of the Lord. Seeking the Kingdom of God is first a process of inward cultivation. You must allow God to work on your intangible traits, thereafter the promise of the physical Kingdom, beholding the pearly gates and the throne becomes fulfilled.

God's promises for your life are sure. Start by seeking first His Kingdom and His righteousness all these things will be added unto you (Matt6:33). Whatever you need… '*the things*', they are available to you when you begin to seek *first* the Kingdom of God.

2. Seek the Lord

> '**Seek the Lord** *and all His strength,*
> *Seek His face continually'*
> *(1 Chronicles 16:11)*

In traditional churches in South Africa we have hymnals 'Ama- xilongo' (*Hyms*) in isi-Xhosa or 'Difela tsa Sione'

(Songs of Zion) in Southern Sotho. These are normally sung during the church service stanza by stanza. In my early days I would go to church without a Bible, let alone the hymn book. I would sometimes deliberately come late to church knowing where 'they are in the programme!' *Mercy*! One day the Lord rebuked me for my behaviour and instructed me to come to His house with His tools. So I started carrying my Bible and a hymn book to church! An interesting thing happened as we sang the songs, they had new meaning. I was illuminated and new revelations came from the same songs I had been singing since my childhood. The routine that I got into to jounce to the beat dissolved as we sang stanza by stanza. I realised that the writers of these hymns had deep revelation... showing that they spent time meditating upon the scriptures. When one reads the Psalms, one realises that the depth, insight and revelation did not come from just shepherding but from extended time in God's presence.

Seeking the Lord is about spending time in His presence. It is about dedicating time in knowing Him. He allows you the opportunity to have intimate fellowship with Him. In dedicating time with Him you grow in the knowledge of Him. In order to spend time seeking the Lord, it is important to set time aside. Develop a routine of how you will schedule time to be with the Lord. For instance, if you wake up at 5AM, ensure that the first hour of your day is set aside to reading the Bible and praying. Time with the Lord is fellowship, make it worth your while. In putting time aside for God He promises the following:

Draws closer to you (James 4:8)

'Draw nigh to God, and He will draw nigh to you.'

He promises you will find Him (Deuteronomy 4:29)

'But if thence thou shalt seek the Lord thy God, thou shalt find Him, if thou seek Him with all they heart and with all thy soul'

Lack no good thing (Psalms 34:10)

'The young lions do lack, and suffer hunger; but they that seek the Lord shall not want any good thing'

Rejoicing and Joy (Psalms 105: 3)

'Glory ye in His holy name; let the heart of them rejoice that seek the Lord'

Rains righteousness upon you (Hosea 10:12)

'Sow yourselves in righteousness, reap in mercy, break-up your fallow ground: For it is time to seek the Lord until He come and rain righteousness upon you'

Wisdom and Understanding (Proverbs 28:5)

'...They that seek the Lord understand all things'

Rewards those who diligently seek Him (Hebrews 11:6)

'...He is a rewarder of those that diligently seek Him'

Seeking the Lord opens you up to the different facets of God. You will experience the I AM that I AM (Exodus 3:14). God will be Whoever you need Him to be. Seek Him and see Who He can be to you. If you are sick, He will be Jehovah Rapha. If you are in need, He will be Jehovah Jireh. If you need victory, He will be Jehovah Nissi. If you need abundance, He will be Jehovah El-Shaddai. Seek the Lord and you will experience Him in different ways.

3. Seek the Word

*'By **the Word** of the Lord were the heavens made: and all the host of them by the breath of His mouth (Psalms 33:6)*

The epistle of John starts with the words *'In the beginning was the Word, and the Word was with God and the Word was God...and the Word became flesh and dwelt among us...full of grace and truth'* (John 1:1,14). When you read the Bible in the beginning (Genesis 1), it refers to the world being void without shape or form...then God said: "*Let there be*!" It proves that the world we live in was created by the Word that came from God. Everything that exists was created by the Word. Think about it, if the Word became flesh and dwelt among us, then the Word is Jesus Himself. We can interchangeably refer to the Word as Jesus and Jesus as the Word. Jesus, the Word of God incarnate. How interesting it is to know when you meditate on the Word, you meditate on Jesus!

God instructed Joshua to meditate on the book of the law (the Word) day and night and for Joshua not to have the Word depart from his mouth, by so doing he will have *good* success.

'This book of the law shall not depart out of thy mouth; but thou shalt meditate therein day and night, that thou mayest observe to do according to all that is written therein: for then thou shalt make thy way prosperous, and then thou shalt have good success' (Joshua 1:8)

In our world, there are things that are used as indicators of success such as cars, houses, yachts, private jets, money, status, etc. They say the difference between men and boys, is the size of their toys! All the things are just that…things. However, God promised Joshua that meditating the Word and not letting it depart from his mouth will grant him good success. That sounds counterintuitive, how can meditation and not letting the Word depart from your mouth lead to success? Moreover…good success. But as it is mentioned in the first chapter of John, *'In the beginning was the Word… all things were made by Him and without Him was not anything that was made'* (John 1:1,3).

Meditation upon the Word allows your thoughts to be aligned with His will. God gave us the Old and New Testaments in the same way someone would write the last will testament. In order for our lives to be aligned to His purpose, the Word is fundamental for us to understand His will. The Psalmist says when you meditate upon the Word of God day and night, you will be like a tree planted by the rivers of water that brings forth fruit in his season, his leaf shall not wither and whatsoever he doeth shall prosper.

> '*Blessed is the man that walketh not in the counsel of the ungodly, nor standeth in the way of sinners, nor sitteth in the seat of the scornful. But his delight is in the law of the Lord; and in his law doth he meditate day and night. And he shall be like a tree planted by the rivers of water, that bringeth forth his fruit in his season; his leaf also shall not wither; and whatsoever he doeth shall prosper.' (Psalms 1:1-3).*

In order to ensure that the effort put into obtaining success is not futile, rather go to the Word that created everything since the beginning. In the same way atoms and molecules are the smallest component of an element. The Word is the component out of which all things are made! When you intentionally seek the Word of God, you set in motion the principle of creating your world with your words. If your words are based on the Word of God, then you create your world-aligning it to God's purposes.

May God plant a desire in you to Seek first the Kingdom of God, Seek the Lord, Seek the Word…and see honour bestowed upon you!

Application

1. What are the things you would like to accomplish
   in life? (It can be in any area of your life)

   _____

   _____

   _____

   _____

   _____

   _____

   _____

   _____

   _____

   _____

   _____

   _____

   _____

   _____

   _____

   _____

   _____

   _____

   _____

   _____

   _____

   _____

   _____

   _____

   _____

2. What attributes do you believe God can cultivate in you for you to achieve that what is in your heart?

_____

_____

_____

_____

_____

_____

_____

_____

_____

_____

_____

_____

_____

_____

_____

_____

_____

_____

_____

_____

_____

_____

_____

_____

_____

_____

_____

3. What facet of God would you like to personally experience in your life?

    I want to see God in my life as

    _____

    I want to see God in my life as

    _____

    I want to see God in my life as

    _____

    I want to see God in my life as

    _____

    I want to see God in my life as

    _____

    I want to see God in my life as

    _____

    I want to see God in my life as

    _____

    I want to see God in my life as

    _____

    I want to see God in my life as

    _____

    I want to see God in my life as

    _____

4. Setting time aside to Seek the Lord and to Seek the Word.
    4.1. Commit to having time. It can be spread out throughout the day. For e.g. Monday 05:00-06:00

(Morning), Tuesday (06:30-07:00 (Morning), and 21:00-21:30 (Evening), or intermittent intervals during the day Friday (05:00-05:15, 07:00-07-30,21:00-22:30)

4.2. Schedule time based on your activities.

	Morning	Day	Night
Monday			
Tuesday			
Wednesday			
Thursday			
Friday			
Saturday			
Sunday			

'Under his direction the altars of the Baals were torn down ...These he broke into pieces'
2 Chronicles 34: 4(NIV)

2

Breaking the Altars of the Fathers

When a seed is planted it goes through the process of germination in order for it to start growing. First the root, then a shoot will come up, through time it will develop and produce after the seed. A seed always produces after its own kind. The Greek word for producing after your own kind is *allos*, meaning another (of the same kind). In the same way that families are referred to as family trees, generations are a derivative of the seeds planted by predecessors[iv]. This illustration is somehow indicative of generational patterns. It takes one generation to plant a seed that will yield fruit that generations to come will reap from it. What you see manifesting in the fruit, is indicative of the seed that gave foundation to the tree. Matthew 7:17 states '...*every good tree bears good fruit, but a bad tree bears bad fruit*' (NIV). When you look at the fruit of your family tree, What do you see? Is the fruit good? What legacy have you inherited? What legacy are you leaving behind? The tree is judged by the fruit it bears.

I once watched a show where John Turnipseed was featured. His story was that 34 members of his family were incarcerated at a point for murder. Imagine fathers, sons, uncles, brothers and nephews from the same family in prison. Some of the other family members who were not in prison were involved in prostitution, some on drugs, and some were even pimps. After he got born again, he started reflecting on the family he came from. In his immediate family he went to prison, his father, his son as well as his grandson. He started praying for his family and over the years some changed their ways, descendants were finishing high school and the ones in prison received salvation. He might not have inherited a good seed, but he used the principles of God's word to change the trajectory of his family.

Just contemplate on the legacy you have inherited and the one you are establishing through the decisions you make daily. *'For every tree is known by his own fruit'(Luke 6:44).* The choices you make will have consequences for now and generations to come. What seed are you planting now and what fruit will be yielded from it?

When reading the book of Chronicles and Kings you come across different Kings of Israel. Some yielded good fruit, some did not. Their reigns are documented as a lesson to the children of Israel of what happens to kings that follow the ordinances of the Lord and those that didn't. Some of the kings chose to follow foreign gods and their end was so wretched. God took offence at the sacrifices they made on an altar that was set apart for Him. When God gave Moses the Ten Commandments, He said '*You shall have no other gods before Me*' (Exodus 20:3,ESV). God was explicit that He alone is God and should be worshipped. No foreign altars should be established. Why do altars matter to God?

What is the significance of an altar?

The altar symbolised a place of worship and established spiritual authority[v]. When the patriarchs honoured God, they would establish an altar and make sacrifices unto the Lord. In order to mark a moment of significance, they established an altar unto the Lord. For instance, Noah, Abraham, Isaac, Jacob, Moses and others established altars when honouring God.

Noah

'*Then Noah built an altar to the Lord*' (Genesis 8:20) NIV

Abraham

'*There he built an altar to the Lord, and called upon the name of the Lord.*'(Genesis 12: 7-8) NIV

Isaac

'*Isaac built an altar there, and called upon the name of the Lord*' (Genesis 26:25) NIV

Jacob

'There he built an altar, and called the place El Bethel: because it was there that God revealed Himself to him ...' (Genesis 35:7) NIV

When the children of Israel fought with Amalek, Aaron and Hur held up the hands of Moses on either side, until the sun went down and Israel prevailed. After the children of Israel defeated Amalek, Moses established an altar for the Lord and called it Jehovah Nissi (Exodus 17:15). Jehovah Nissi, meaning the Lord my banner and victory. Through building an altar, Moses established godly spiritual authority. His action was underpinning that, had it not have been for the Lord, Israel would not have prevailed. When the Lord instructed Moses to build the Tabernacle of Meeting, the altar was used by the Levites to offer burnt offerings and sacrifices to the Lord. The altar was a symbolic in establishing godly spiritual authority for the children of Israel.

In the New Covenant, through Jesus dying for us on the cross, we were made holy through the sacrifice of the body of Jesus Christ once and for all (Hebrews 10:10). Jesus Christ connected us to the promises of God, being the ultimate sacrifice for us (Galatians 3:13-14). God ensured that for us godly Spiritual Authority be established through the sacrifice of Jesus Christ. Make sure that a godly altar is established in your life.

Why break down an ungodly altar?

God wants us to worship Him alone. When He gave Moses the Ten Commandments, He further gave instructions on the establishment of altars. *'You shall have no other gods before me ...you shall not make gods of silver to be with me, nor shall you make for yourselves gods of gold. An altar of earth you shall make for me...' (Exodus 20:3,23-24 NIV).* God was explicit that no foreign gods should be worshipped.

Another time was when Solomon completed building the temple, God visited him and instructed him. He told Solomon that should Israel move from His commandments, they will be cut off from the land He gave them and they will be a ridicule among other nations. God appeared to Solomon indicating that Israel will be established as long as they keep the statutes of the God of their forefathers, they will be established (1 Kings 9:6-10). Insomuch as a decree was made for the kings and the nation must follow the ordinances of God, some kings disobeyed God's commands and were cut off or even exiled. The likes of Ahab, Ahaziah and Manasseh are some examples of kings who did evil in the sight of the Lord.

Ahab

'And Ahab the son of Omri did evil in the sight of the Lord above all that were before him... that he took to wife Jezebel

the daughter of Ethbaal king of the Zidonians, and went and served Baal, and worshipped him...' (1 Kings 16:30-32)

Ahaziah

'Ahaziah the son of Ahab began to reign over Israel... And he did evil in the sight of the Lord, and walked in the way of his father, and in the way of his mother, and in the way of Jeroboam the son of Nebat, who made Israel to sin: For he served Baal, and worshipped him, and provoked to anger the Lord God of Israel, according to all that his father had done.' (1 Kings 22:51-53)

Manasseh

'Manasseh ... he did evil in the eyes of the Lord, following the detestable practices of the nations the Lord had driven out before the Israelites...he erected altars to the Baals... he built altars in the temple of the Lord' (2 Chronicles 33:1-4) NIV

When you follow the subsequent results of the kings who worshipped Baal, their end was tragic. They were cut off, exiled and lost their glory. Insomuch as there were kings that did evil, the voice of God still went forth through his prophets. With all the wickedness that was going on the voice of God would provide warnings. During the reign of King Jeroboam, it was prophesied that Josiah will be king. He will rise and re-establish an altar for the Lord.

'... And he cried against the altar in the word of the Lord, and said, O altar, altar, thus saith the Lord; Behold, a child shall be born unto the house of David, Josiah by name; and upon thee shall he offer the priests of the high places that burn incense upon thee...'(1 Kings 13:1-2).

Jeroboam's wickedness transcended into the reigns of many kings that God detested. Amon the son of Manasseh, was another king who did not walk in the ordinances of God and God removed him. His son, Josiah reigned in his stead from the age of eight, as it was prophesied (1 Kings 13:1-2). When Josiah took over, he rededicated Israel to the Lord. His predecessors had established an ungodly spiritual authority for Israel by worshiping foreign gods.

Josiah was intent on re-establishing the altar of the Lord. He had no mercy when breaking down the altars of his fathers. He began to purge Judah and Jerusalem from the high places. He broke down every altar, every idol in pieces and made dust of them. He had understanding that leave no stone unturned when destroying the ungodly altar. He changed the trajectory of Israel and re-established the authority of God through the altar.

'... And they chopped down the altars of the Baals in his presence, and he cut down the incense altars that stood above them. And he broke in pieces the Asherim and the carved and the metal images, and he made dust of them ...' (2 Chronicles 34:3-4) ESV.

Insomuch as you might not know the altar established in your family, evaluate the fruit. A tree is judged by the fruit it bears. The fruit can help you identify the seed it is derived from. Get real when evaluating the fruit. Ask the relevant questions. For instance, how many children in your family are growing up knowing and living with their fathers, from your current generation to the forefathers? How many family members are in prison at any given time? How prevalent is abuse in your family (physical, sexual, emotional)? How many members are serving and living for God? How many have established families, businesses or careers? Ask pertinent questions.

By examining the fruit, it is a good step to reflect and see what altar has been established for your family. Become honest with the fruit you see manifesting through the generations. If you see the fruit pleasing then bless God. An altar for the Lord has been established. Carry on with the legacy you inherited and ensure that the decisions you make will transcend generations to come. In the event you are not entirely proud of the fruit, truthfully examine the altar. If, like Josiah you see that what was promised to you by God's word is not coherent with your lineage, make a decision to break down any ungodly altars.

By so doing, you become a new seed and generations to come will be derived from the seeds you are planting by the decisions you make. You can choose to spiritually break down every ungodly altar, every idol and like Josiah, you can make dust of it. Be zealous and leave no stone unturned, literally. You are the new seed! When generations to come will examine the fruit that will be yielded from your seed...it will be a by-product of the godly altar that you have established.

When my brother started intentionally building godly altars, it was in 2003 after we attended the 50th wedding anniversary of Rev. Andrew and Cathy (Pelonomi) Makhene, who have both gone to be with the Lord. It was beautiful to witness. That occasion inspired hope that being rooted in the Lord you become sustained, preserved and kept. You could see the trans-generational blessing as the generations gathered. He began to study about Josiah and intentionally established godly altars in order to see the trans-generational blessing in our family.

How to establish an altar for the Lord?

1. Be Born Again

'Marvel not, that I say unto thee: Ye must be born again' (John 3:7).

Accepting Jesus as your personal Lord and saviour is pertinent to establishing an altar for the Lord. By confessing with your mouth, believing in your heart that God raised Him from the dead, you are saved.

'That if thou shalt confess with thy mouth the Lord Jesus, and shalt believe in thine heart that God hath raised him from the dead, thou shalt be saved.' (Romans 10:9)

How can something so simple change the trajectory of one's life and family, for now and eternity? Jesus says in Matthew 15:13: *'Every plant which my heavenly Father hath not planted, shall be rooted up'*. In other words, once you are in Him, every seed that is contrary to God's will that was planted, even before your time, will be uprooted. We've established that a good seed produces good fruit, how much better that He, the Ancient of Days re-establishes the seed in your lineage? The Bible further states: *'Therefore if any man be in Christ, he is a new creature: old things are passed away; behold, all things are become new'* (2 Corinthians 5:17). God will make all things new in your life.

2. Cultivate the fruit of the Spirit

Second step, work on cultivating the fruit of the Spirit. The fruit of the Spirit talk about building and establishing character. Our character is who we are on a day to day basis. Who we are daily affects our decisions and ultimately our destiny. We say the fruit, not *fruits* as all the fruit emanate from love. In order to see the manifestation of the fruit of the Spirit, one must be led by the Spirit of God.

Galatians 5:22-23,25

'But the fruit of the Spirit is love, joy, peace, longsuffering, gentleness, goodness, faith, meekness, temperance: against such, there is no law...If we live by the Spirit let us also walk in the Spirit'

Love

'...God is love...' (1 John 4:16)

Love is the first fruit of the Spirit. If God is love, then *ceteris paribus* love is God. First start with Love Himself, then the other fruit will manifest. A revelation of love casts out all fear(1 John 4:16). Walking in love removes the fear that underpins negative perceptions and emotions.

Joy

'...For the joy of the Lord is your strength' (Nehemiah 8:10)

The joy *of the Lord* is exactly that...it's His joy! Pursue to understand His joy and what makes Him joyous. His joy is seeing us embrace the victory we have in Him! In having a revelation of His joy, we don't look at what makes us joyous, but it is in His joy in that we are strengthened in all circumstances. May the joy of the Lord be your strength in times of weakness and discouragement!

Peace

'Great peace have they which love thy law: and nothing shall offend them' (Ps119:165)

Peace, is God's shalom. Shalom in Hebrew means peace where nothing missing and nothing is broken. It speaks of peace that is beyond human understanding that covers you. Peace creates a pleasant atmosphere and enables amicable resolution in case of conflict. May that be your portion!

Longsuffering (Endurance)

'...*He that shall endure till the end, the same shall be saved*' *(Mark 13:13)*

When going through trials and are being tested you will need to endure and hold on to the profession of your faith. When Jesus hung on the cross, He endured such that redemption's plan is fulfilled. Hold on to your faith and endure until the end… no matter what!

Gentleness

'...*I Paul, myself beseech you by the meekness and gentleness of Christ*' *(2 Corinthians 10:1)*

During times when your limits are tested, acting out in gentleness will continually work on cultivating this fruit of the Spirit. Gentleness speaks of being outwardly soft. Be gentle despite how others react towards you.

Goodness (kindness)

'...*That I may show him kindness for Jonathan's sake*' *(2 Samuel 9:1)*

Acting out goodness to those deserving and undeserving. Those who may have hurt you, treat them with kindness.

Outwardly do random acts of kindness and be a blessing. We are blessed to be blessings, that is a higher life.

Faith

'Now the just shall live by faith. If any man draw back, my soul shall have no pleasure in him' (Hebrews 10:38)

Faith is more than subscribing to a religion. Faith is taking God's word, believing it and confessing it despite the circumstance. The just (righteous) shall live by faith. Believe God's word until you see what you believed and confessed manifests.

Meekness

'...But the meek shall inherit the earth and shall delight themselves in the abundance of peace' (Psalms 37:11)

Some people mistake meekness for weakness. Meekness is an attribute that speaks of being cloaked with humility. There is a strength that comes to being meek and humble, God gives grace to the humble[vi].

Temperance (self-control)

'He that hath no rule over his own spirit is like a city that is broken down and without walls' (Proverbs 25:28)

Temperance speaks of being self-controlled. The analogy in Proverbs 25:28, alludes one without control over his spirit is like a city without walls. Walls provided protection for the city. Having self-control guards your heart, your emotions should not get out of control that you end up regretting your actions. Like a city with walls, have self control.

3. Dedicate time to Fast and Pray over your lineage

Prayer and fasting allows God to be part of charting a new trajectory for your life and that of your family. In the seventeenth Chapter of Matthew, after Jesus descended the mountain of transfiguration, His Disciples met with Him frantic that they could not cast out demons from a boy. After casting out the demon, the Disciples asked Him, how was it possible the He cast out the demon and they could not. He responded to them and said '...*Nothing shall be impossible for you...howbeit this kind goeth not out but by prayer and fasting*' (Matthew 17:20-21).

When looking at your family tree and there are things to uproot, it will take more than the 20 second *grace* prayer that is said over the food. Dedicate time to fast and pray. Find pertinent scriptures to stand on and remind God of His promises that should be fulfilled over your life and that of your family.

When Daniel was in Babylon, he read the writings of the Prophet Jeremiah. The word of the Lord said after seventy years in Babylon, God will grant the children of Israel deliverance from captivity.

'This is what the Lord says, "When seventy years are completed for Babylon, I will come to you and fulfil my good promise to bring you back to this place. For I know the plans I have for you," declares the Lord, "plans to prosper you and not to harm you, plans to give you hope and a future"' (Jeremiah 29:10-11) NIV

While he was in Babylon, this promise was not yet fulfilled after the said seventy years. Daniel declared a fast to pray such that the promises of God for the nation to be fulfilled (Dan 9: 1-17).

'... I Daniel understood from the Scriptures, according to the word of the Lord given to Jeremiah the prophet, that the desolation of Jerusalem would last seventy years'. (Daniel 9:2) NIV

In the same way like Daniel, seek the scriptures and see God's promises for your life. Declare a fast and pray for God to intervene on your behalf and your lineage! Pray until you see the fulfilment of God's promises.

4. Repent for the sins of your Fathers and Purge

There is a saying *'in order to know where you are going you have to know where you come from'*. If your father is a king, then you know that you are of royalty. You cannot be seen doing ignoble acts as the blood that runs through your veins is that of a monarch. You need to know whose blood runs through your veins. We all come from somewhere, there is a lineage we are all affiliated to. Sometimes, scrutinising your family tree you might look at your predecessors in a disparaging way. There might be some things you are not entirely proud of. There is no need to be ashamed! We are all born in the families we are born in so that God is able to fulfil His purposes through you and your family. When Matthew chronicles the genealogy of Jesus, not everyone enlisted has an impeccable record (Matt 1). However, God still used everyone through the generations to ensure that through their existence humanity's redemption plan can be fulfilled. Jesus came through a lineage of imperfect people. God had to fulfil what He said in the garden of Eden that the seed of a woman would bruise the head of the serpent (Genesis 3:15). God follows through on His word. A decision that you take for God, will transcend generations. He will watch over His word to perform it in your life (Jeremiah 1:12).If we confess our sins God is faithful and just to forgive (1 John 1:9). Bring all past iniquities to the Lord and He will work it out and turn things around.

Repent, repent, repent! Repent for any altars that may have been established that are contrary to God's word. Repenting entails doing an about turn. When looking at a compass for instance there are two polarised directions, North and South. If you make an about turn it is like making a 180° turn in the opposite direction. Repent, make an about turn, go towards God's ordinances and His purpose will be fulfilled in your life and that of your family!

Purge, purge, purge! Purging entails denouncing and ridding your life of anything that is not aligned to God's word. Be aggressive like Josiah, break them down to dust and purge (2 Chronicles 34:4). Josiah 'made dust of them', meaning he left behind no residue of the ungodly altars. Believe and use the authority of the name of Jesus when praying.

5. Believe God has heard your prayers

God is a prayer answering God! Have confidence that when you present your prayers to Him, he hears and He answers.

'And this is the confidence that we have in Him, that, if we ask any thing according to his will, He heareth us' (1 John 5:14)

Praying according to His will is praying according to His Word. Break down ungodly altars so that God will receive your prayers. In Revelations Chapter 8, it describes that in Heaven, on the golden altar before the throne, the prayers of the saints are like a sweet smelling incense before the Lord.

'And another angel came and stood at the altar, having a golden censer; and there was given unto him much incense, that he should offer it with the prayers of all saints upon the golden altar which was before the throne. And the smoke of the incense, which came with the prayers of the saints, ascended up before God out of the angel's hand.' (Revelations 8:3-4)

May your prayers be counted among them those of the saints…as new godly altars are established!

Application

1. List the good things that run in your family.

_____

_____

_____

_____

_____

_____

_____

_____

_____

_____

_____

_____

_____

_____

_____

_____

_____

_____

_____

_____

_____

_____

_____

_____

_____

_____

_____

2. List the things you are not proud of that run in your family

_____

_____

_____

_____

_____

_____

_____

_____

_____

_____

_____

_____

_____

_____

_____

_____

_____

_____

_____

_____

_____

_____

_____

_____

_____

3. What things would you like to see change in your family?

_____

_____

_____

_____

_____

_____

_____

_____

_____

_____

_____

_____

_____

_____

_____

_____

_____

_____

_____

_____

_____

_____

_____

_____

_____

_____

4. What daily decisions are you going to make that future generations can benefit from?

_____

_____

_____

_____

_____

_____

_____

_____

_____

_____

_____

_____

_____

_____

_____

_____

_____

_____

_____

_____

_____

_____

_____

_____

5. What verses you will stand on praying for your family?

_____

_____

_____

_____

_____

_____

_____

_____

_____

_____

_____

_____

_____

_____

_____

_____

_____

_____

_____

_____

_____

_____

_____

_____

_____

_____

_____

6. How do you see your family in years to come?

_____

_____

_____

_____

_____

_____

_____

_____

_____

_____

_____

_____

_____

_____

_____

_____

_____

_____

_____

_____

_____

_____

_____

_____

_____

_____

_____

'I beseech ye therefore, bretheren, by the mercies of God that ye present your bodies a living sacrifice, holy, acceptable unto God, which is your reasonable service'
(Romans 12:1)

3

Living Sacrifices

Tabloids make a lot of money, especially when a scandal is published. Men of great stature in ministry, sports, business and politics have their reputations tarnished once a disgraceful story breaks out. In the event of a sex scandal, the sleuths will be on the prowl looking for a scoop. A tumultuous season unfolds as surreptitious details are laid bare in the court of public opinion. The consequences thereafter are dire in terms of reputation and family life. The difference between the famous men and the others of similar stories in society, is that some of the stories did not find a publisher neither did they get caught. It is the 'small things' that get people caught. There is a sin that easily entangles and it can bring one's life to ruin, if not dealt with. The Apostle Paul writes that we must set aside the sin that so easily entangles us (Hebrews 12:1, NIV).

What is *that* sin in your life? You may have built up all your defences, then there's this one sin that just takes you back! Discover that sin that easily entangles you. Is it your ego? Is it succumbing to peer pressure? Is it lying about your real life status? Is it pornography? Is it looking at other options on the menu, even though the main course has been served (i.e. lust or a roving eye even if you are married)? Whatever it is, ask the Holy Spirit to help you identify the sin that easily entangles. Leaving it for the future will only result in a higher price to pay at a later stage in life. Bishop Mosa Sono once said *"If you leave it for later, the price is always greater."* The men who make the scandalous headlines did not start on the day the scandals broke out. It could have been small iterations of sin that culminated to the point of causing public shame.

Discrete things done in moderation in secret ultimately become visible in public. But imagine the inverse of that. In moderation, allowing the word of God to deal with that easily entangling sin. You can start by cutting out vile talk, gradually changing habits or even moving away from bad company. The result will be made public for all to see. The Psalmist says *'Thy word I have hidden in my heart that I may not sin against thee'* (Ps 119: 11). Allow the word of God to be the foundation for new thoughts, new talks, new habits, new character…ultimately a new life! It is amazing that when Jesus taught His Disciples to pray, He mentioned to them going to their closet and pray in secret and the Father will reward them openly (Matthew 6:6). A public display is a reward of what was done in secret.

Preserving Sexual Purity and Fleeing Fornication and Adultery

When it comes to the power of preserving sexual purity, the life of Samson comes to mind. Yes, that Samson who was with Delilah! It wouldn't be fair to evaluate his life simply by observing what happened in the end of his story, whereas his beginning was nothing short of a miracle of God. The thing about Samson is that he was a Nazirite. That means he was separated to God, set apart, or consecrated so to speak, from birth. The instruction to his mother was that his head was not to be shaved, he should not drink wine or beer, and not to eat anything unclean (Judges 13). A Nazirite would make a vow to consecrate themselves unto God. Samson was able to do great exploits for God as the Spirit of the Lord was upon him as a result of the Nazirite vow (Judges 13:25,14:6). In the days of Moses, a person (male or female) could make a Nazirite vow, similar to that of Samson in order to separate themselves for God's service (Numbers 6:1-5). Samson was consecrated and set apart for God from birth. However, he violated the Nazirite vow by sleeping around with prostitutes and Philistine women.

Samson taking a Philistine wife

'And Samson went down to Timnath, and saw a woman in Timnath of the daughters of the Philistines. And he came up, and told his father and his mother, and said, I have seen a woman in

Timnath of the daughters of the Philistines: now therefore get her for me to wife' (Judges 14:1-2)

Samson with a prostitute

'Samson went to Gaza, and there he saw a prostitute, and he went in to her.' (Judges 16:1)

Samson with Delilah

'After this he loved a woman in the Valley of Sorek, whose name was Delilah' (Judges 16:4)

Similarly, like Samson, when we get born again, we become separated unto God. We were redeemed, bought by the blood of Jesus and are set apart. *'For ye are bought with a price: therefore glorify God in your body, and in your spirit, which are God's' (1 Cor 6:20).* Samson took for granted what God gave him. One night of pleasure with Delilah cost him his sight and strength. Above everything, it cost him his Nazirite vow. He thought he could carry on as usual…but unbeknownst to him, the strength he thought he had, had departed.

'Then she called "Samson, the Philistines are upon you!" He awoke from his sleep and thought, "I'll go out as before and shake myself free." But he did not know that the Lord had left him' (Judges 16:20) NIV

The lesson to be learned from Samson is that protect that which God has given you through the gift of salvation.

Don't be frivolous with what God has gifted you with – regardless of what it may be. The Apostle Paul in 1 Corinthians 6 reminds us that our bodies are for the Lord and the temple of the Holy Ghost.

'... *Now the body is not for fornication, but for the Lord; and the Lord for the body...' (1 Corinthians 6:13)*

'Flee sexual immorality. All other sins a person commits are outside the body, but whoever sins sexually sins against their own body. Do you not know that your bodies are temples of the Holy Spirit, who is in you, whom you have received from God? You are not your own, you are bought at a price. Therefore honor God with your bodies' (1 Corinthians 6:,18-20 NIV).

The Bible implores us that we ought to present our bodies holy and acceptable to God and to use our bodies to the glory of God. When my brother passed on at the age of thirty, he was still a virgin. This was truly God's grace upon his life. It is possible for a man to keep himself sexually pure. We were bought with a high price and with every ounce of our being spirit, soul and body- God should be glorified. Jesus paid a high price for your redemption, honour Him with your body!

The fifth Chapter of Proverbs is metaphorical. It is a warning against adultery, but also gives advice about enjoying marriage. In the preceding verses (Proverbs 5:1-14), Solomon describes the subsequent destructive results of adultery and lusts of the flesh. He also warns of the outcome of such a life. Verse 9 states '*Lest you lose your honour to others and your dignity'.* Furthermore in verse 11 it states *'at the end of your life you will groan, when your flesh and body are spent' (NIV).* This alludes to *Casanova*, or promiscuous ways lead to leaving your dignity with others and at the end of it all your flesh spent, or wasted. It may seem fun to be a 'player', boasting about the conquests between the sheets, but the book of Proverbs likens that to a wasted life. Look at the scandals that break out, men with illustrious careers lose their prestige instantaneously- that can be equivalent to 'wasting' one's life. When all is said and done reminiscing on life will be groans and regrets. Solomon forewarns that the ultimate consequence for this lifestyle is losing your soul in hell (Proverbs 5:5). Having said that, God provides forgiveness in all situations. His forgiveness is like a reset button of a computer. Once forgiven, you are reset to original settings. Receive His forgiveness so that He can rewrite your story and restore your honour and dignity.

In the latter part of this chapter Solomon illustrates the following: *'waters from your own cistern', 'rejoice with the wife of thy youth', 'let her breasts satisfy thee at all times', 'my son, why be intoxicated with another man's wife'.* Furthermore he explains, that they (waters) must be your own, and not strangers' *(Proverbs 5:15-21).* Meaning, the best place to experience sexual pleasure is from your own wife. May it be that, that which God has bestowed upon your life is not cast out like waters in the streets! Take lessons from Samson, be faithful to your Nazirite vow and do not lose your strength, honour and dignity to strangers.

In the event whereby you may have erred and stumbled, return to God and repent. Allow God to help you, He is a gracious God! Samson in the end did just that. He sought help from the Lord to regain his strength. God restored him and the Philistines that ridiculed him were destroyed (Judges 16:28-31). God is merciful and kind, He can restore you once again, just give Him a chance to do so.

Pornography and Sexting

There is no explicit commandment that states *'Thou shalt not watch or text X-rated content'*. Inasmuch as this is true, the Bible is still relevant in terms of the way we ought to conduct ourselves. Some men have become so addicted to X-rated content that these secret pleasures make them unfaithful not only to their spouses, but also to themselves. How does one get rid of the addiction, or shake off bad habits? How does one deal genuinely with sexual addictions without feeling judged or condemned?

The place to start in learning to manage addictions or bad habits, is taking care of the thoughts. It sounds easier said than done, but it is a starting point. Go through a sifting process before acting upon anything. Before anyone clicks on a link or types 'www', or even engages in elicit conversations, it starts with a thought. Proverbs 23:7 *'For as he thinketh in his heart, so is he'*. What is contemplated upon becomes acted upon. What you think about shapes who you are! In order to curb and tame thoughts, someone once said that in the middle of an argument, allow a 10 second pause before responding. This allows time to think of the reaction and ultimately acting in a way you won't regret afterwards. In the same way, pause and sift the thoughts before taking action.

'Finally, brethren, whatsoever things are true, whatsoever things are honest, whatsoever things are just, whatsoever things are pure, whatsoever things are lovely, whatsoever things are of good report; if there be any virtue, and if there be any praise, think on these things.' (Philippians 4:8)

Prior to engaging in any thought or action, try this sifting process:

Is it true?

Is it honest?

Is it pure?

Is it lovely?

Is it of good report?

Is there any virtue?

Is there any praise?

If so, you think on it! The sifting process allows curbing thoughts that will lead to actions of regret. Get the thought process right and the right actions will follow.

Masturbating

One day when we attended a Youth meeting at our church we were being taught about sex. The sub-topic was masturbation. Our Youth leaders invited one of our Pastors, Mpumi Mthembu, to address us. She took such a different angle to the topic that left an indelible mark in our hearts. She requested that for just ten seconds we look at our hands, study them and observe every contour, see how God made them. She spoke about 'The purpose of hands'.

Hands are intricate parts of our bodies. Behind the skin there are sinews, muscles, bones, cartilage and nerves. God perfectly designed them to have so many uses. They build. They hold. They craft. They design. They protect. They bless.

When we look at the earth we say it is the work of God's hands. When a baby is born, fathers take pride in holding the little one in their hands. Hand-shakes often affirm business deals. When a couple gets married they hold hands and put on rings as a sign of covenant. In the Old Testament when Isaac blessed Jacob he laid hands on him.

'And Isaac said unto Jacob, Come near, I pray thee, that I may feel thee, my son, whether thou be my very son Esau or not. ... because his hands were hairy, as his brother Esau's hands: so he blessed him'(Genesis 27:21,27).

The Levites were instructed to wash their hands (and feet) when they entered the tent of meeting.

'For Aaron and his sons shall wash their hands and their feet thereat: When they go into the tabernacle....' (Exodus 30:19-20)

When we worship God we raise our hands to him.

'...I have lift up mine hand unto the Lord, the most high God, the possessor of heaven and earth' (Genesis 14:22)

The point was made ... hands have a purpose. Miles Munroe said *"where purpose is not defined, abuse is inevitable."* Abuse is synonymous with misuse. Imagine the same hands being used for something contrary to their purpose. We were taught to understand the purpose of our hands and use them to the glory of God. May your hands not be used contrary to their purpose. Know the purpose of your hands, so that in His presence you unabashedly raise holy hands in worship!

Make a vow with your eyes

God made all things beautiful. After creation, He looked at it and said: *'It is good!'* Everything around us should be for us to ponder on the splendour of His handiworks. With that said, what we see with our eyes is not harmful, how it is processed is what will make it harmful. Job says *'I made a covenant with my eyes not to look lustfully at a girl' (Job 31:1,NIV).* Sometimes you cannot help what you see, however guard your thinking process such that what you see does not cause you to sin in your heart! Proverbs 23:33 says *'Thine eyes shall behold strange women and thine heart shall utter perverse things.'* Make a vow with your eyes not to look lustfully at a woman. Make a vow not to be in conversations that objectify women. Make a vow not watch any media that demeans women. It is a vow you can make to guard your heart with all diligence for out of it are the issues of life (Proverbs 4:23).

Jesus said: *'If thine eye offend thee, pluck it out...it is better for thee to enter the kingdom of God with one eye than having two eyes and be cast into hell fire'* (Matthew 18:9). If this had to be applied literally, a lot of people would walk around with pirate patches! Jesus is speaking of being aggressive in dealing with what we see. He is also giving perspective that one day we will account to God. So with every lustful look, there is a God to account to. Make a vow with your eyes, a vow that will save you from hell fire.

No Hold on Me

One thing we know as children of God is that, no matter how devoted we can be, the prince of the world is coming to attack. Paul calls it 'the evil day' (Ephesians 6:13). To everyone, there will be an evil day. Do not worry, Jesus promises us victory. When the enemy comes to attack, does he have a hold on you? Jesus said:*'...the prince of this world is coming. He has no hold over me'(John 14:30,NIV).* Someone who has a hold on you can claim you have something that belongs to them. They can make demands on you at any given time. When Satan comes looking for his stuff, would he find anything hidden in your possession? What hold will he have on you? Is there anything in your possession that belongs to him? If you have anything that belongs to him, he will use it manipulate, blackmail and intimidate you.

Holding someone's possessions, reminds me of Rachel Jacob's wife. After serving Laban for twenty years, Jacob decided to flee with his wives in the middle of the night. Their abrupt departure was because Laban had changed Jacob's wages ten times, cheated him and his attitude towards him had changed. He took Rachel and Leah, his wives, and all his possessions. As they went, Rachel went to steal her father's household gods while Laban was sheering his sheep. Laban pursued Jacob and caught up with him, accusing him of leaving abruptly and stealing his gods. Laban searched Jacob's tents looking for his gods. Unbeknownst to them both, that Rachel had stolen them. They did not find them as she hid the gods. Jacob pronounced a curse that whoever stole them must die! (Gen 31:1-55). When Rachel gave birth to Benjamin, she died while giving birth (Gen 35:18).

Looking at the story of the stolen gods of Laban, Rachel held on to the household gods instead of following the Lord God of her husband Jacob. She lied about the possession of the gods she stole. Examine your life. Is there anything the devil can use against you? Do you still have the phone number of that girl who causes you to fall? Do you secretly go on drinking binges? Do you maybe have anger issues that are still unresolved? Is there a corrupt business deal lurking somewhere? Do you abuse your wife and nobody knows? Many scenarios can be played out that entail 'having the devil's stuff!

Galatians 5:19-22, speaks of the works of the flesh. These are acts of the carnal nature that work against what the Spirit of God is cultivating in your spirit.

'Now the works of the flesh are evident: sexual immorality, impurity, sensuality, idolatry, sorcery, enmity, strife, jealousy, fits of anger, rivalries, dissensions, divisions, envy, drunkenness, orgies, and things like these. I warn you, as I warned you before, that those who do such things will not inherit the kingdom of God' (ESV)

Rid your life of the works of the flesh. Rid your life of anything that will cause him to manipulate and blackmail you. When Satan comes, be firm, rebuke him and tell him: *'Satan, you have NO hold on me!'*

The Apostle Paul makes a request that we present our bodies as living sacrifices, holy and acceptable to God as an act of worship to Him(Rom 12:1). A sacrifice can refer to what the Levites offered at the altar. Remember God that God is a holy God (Lev 11:45). When coming into His presence we should come washed and cleansed by the blood of Jesus. As a form of worship bring our bodies as living sacrifices. Continually deal with the sins that easily entangle…Make a vow with your eyes, flee fornication and have the confidence to raise holy hands…being a living sacrifice set apart for God's use!

Application: Dealing with Addictions/ Destructive Habits

1. Do you have any hidden addictions/ destructive habits that you are struggling to shake off?

_____

_____

_____

_____

_____

_____

_____

_____

_____

_____

_____

_____

_____

_____

_____

_____

_____

_____

_____

_____

_____

_____

_____

_____

2. What action (s) are you willing to take to deal with the habit/addiction?

_____

_____

_____

_____

_____

_____

_____

_____

_____

_____

_____

_____

_____

_____

_____

_____

_____

_____

_____

_____

_____

_____

_____

_____

_____

3. Can you identify a brother (s) / spiritual leader(s) you can confide in to help deal with your addiction/habit? *Have an accountability partner. Someone you can account to as you are on a journey to recovery*

_____

_____

_____

_____

_____

_____

_____

_____

_____

_____

_____

_____

_____

_____

_____

_____

_____

_____

_____

_____

_____

_____

4. Develop a Prayer plan. Find verses that apply to your situation and allow God to work in you standing on His word to transform you.

_____

_____

_____

_____

_____

_____

_____

_____

_____

_____

_____

_____

_____

_____

_____

_____

_____

_____

_____

_____

_____

_____

_____

_____

_____

_____

5. Monitor your success (for e.g. 1 month, 3 weeks and 4 hours I haven't visited a porn site)

_____

_____

_____

_____

_____

_____

_____

_____

_____

_____

_____

_____

_____

_____

_____

_____

_____

_____

_____

_____

_____

_____

_____

_____

_____

_____

'...you will know how people ought to conduct themselves'
(1 Timothy 3:15, NIV)

4

Behind the Suit

In Tyler Perry's movie '*The Diary of a Mad Black Woman*', there is a scene where Charles McCarter, a Defence attorney is with his client. Charles' client is a drug dealer on trial for killing a police officer, and there is video evidence. During a court recess, they have a conversation and the client threatens him. Charles responds by saying '*Don't let the suit fool you!*' The interpretation for us was, even though a man might be wearing a bespoke well fitted suit and smelling with good cologne... Who is the man behind the suit?

Are you the type of guy who is polite to waiters? Do you have any regard for the beggar on the street? When people protest for a cause that doesn't affect you personally, are you empathetic towards their plight? Do you show affection to your mom, wife and sister? More than what you drive...what drives you? Have you ever considered the attitude you project and how you are perceived?

The saying goes *manners maketh the man.* When was the last time you saw someone stand up for a lady or the elderly on the bus or subway? When was the last time you saw someone courteously allow another driver in traffic? The last time you saw someone open a door for a lady? Apparently if you see a guy opening the door for a lady either the relationship or the car is new! Rather than asking about a proverbial *'someone'*...when was the last time you did random acts of kindness? Random acts of kindness should not be a taboo, chivalry still needs to be demonstrated in our days. Courtesy and kindness are still traits that need to be outwardly demonstrated. They set apart gentlemen from the rest! If you haven't been actively being courteous, it takes 21 days to develop a habit. Be cognisant of opportunities that present themselves, leading you to developing the character of a man cut above the rest. If people showed a little more kindness, a little more courtesy...Can you imagine how that could transform our world?

Attitude of Servitude

When thinking of servants in our era roles such as waiters, hotel staff, parking attendants, etc. come to mind. In Biblical times servants would serve their masters. In the event a master had travelling guests they would wash the feet as a sign of welcoming them and prepare meals as they were of service to them. Imagine how reprehensible it is to wash someone's feet who has been travelling in the desert for a few days! Jesus said *'But he that is greatest among you shall be your servant'* (Matthew 23:11). Those that serve others, Jesus regards them as the greatest. The paradox is that those who do the lowliest work are regarded as the greatest! Jesus is onto something…take heed! Life provides different avenues to serve. Find an opportunity to be a servant!

Serving your Family

When God wants to bless a nation, He starts first with a family. When He blessed the nation of Israel, he started with Abraham's family.

'Moreover He said, I am the God of thy father, the God of Abraham, the God of Isaac, and the God of Jacob' (Exodus 3:6)

The family is an important nucleus where the first contact with love happens. Families are not perfect and there can visible anomalies in some. There can be family feuds, estate disputes and lack of concern for one another. You can find that through disagreements people are forced to 'choose sides', this causes deep relational issues. You can make a difference in your family. God wants us to start in our families so that it can be a ripple effect on society. You can serve your family in several ways.

Be a Unifier

In the event of a family dispute, are you the cause of it, in the middle of it or are you inclined to take sides? Family feuds can be so painful that they mar the gift family is.

Being around family can end being just a burden and a root of pain for some. In Psalms 133:1-3 it says *'Behold, how good and how pleasant it is for brethren to dwell together in unity! ...for <u>there</u> the Lord commanded the blessing, even life for evermore.'* The blessing is *there* where there is unity. Refuse to be a family gossip monger. Take a stand not to be in the cause of feuds. Be a lateral thinker, view all points of view and seek to find amicable solutions in your family feuds. The blessing of God comes when there is unity. Choose a different path such that the blessing is experienced in your family.

Be a Peacemaker

'Blessed are the peacemakers: for they shall be called the children of God' (Matthew 5:9). Jesus said these words as part of the sermon on the mount. In order for someone to make peace, there must have been conflict. When you are faced with situations of disputes, opt to be on the side of peace. To reflect the God in you be the one who brings peace. If in your home there is an atmosphere of arguments, seek amicable ways to resolve it. If your sister does not speak to you, try call her. If your father does not make time for you, take the initiative to see him. If your mother has abandoned you, be the one who forgives. You could say *"Oh you don't know how they have hurt me! It's gone on for so long, what is the point?"* The point is not about the next person, it is about you in pursuit of peace.

'Therefore if thine enemy hunger, feed him; if he thirst, give him drink: for in so doing thou shalt heap coals of fire on

his head. Be not overcome of evil, but overcome evil with good '(Romans 25:20-21).

My brother once said: *"Don't fight fire with fire, fight fire with a fire extinguisher!"* Show love and extend peace, even to those who don't reciprocate it. The promise is sure...be a *peacemaker* and you *shall* be called a child of God!

Belong

There is an innate need for humans to belong. After a tragic occurrence, my dad would stretch out his hands, give a group hug and say *"We belong together."* Belonging is an integral part of who we are. God provides families that nobody should be isolated.

'God setteth the solitary in families' (Psalms 68:6).

Different circumstances can occur whereby one is orphaned, abandoned and really be alone. In a situation like that, look at the provision from God of the immediate nucleus that may resemble a family. It can be institutions, foster homes, churches etc. Even in that, you are not alone. Trust God that despite your background He will fulfil His word and you will be planted in a family.

If you are blessed with the gift of family, be supportive. Conduct random visits, especially to the elders. When you heard of a hospitalisation give a courtesy call or even go and visit. Attend the weddings and the parties. Just be there. Your presence will give the sense of belonging. I admire how African families as well as Italians intentionally invest in family relations. In Italy they say *'La famiglia e tutto'*- simply meaning *'Family is everything.'* Make time for family…just belong. Family is a gift!

Serving God

In case you are looking for a place where there are always vacancies, God Inc. is always on the look-out for Soul Winners and servants. The gospel of Mark 16:30 states *'…Go ye into all the world, and preach the gospel to every creature. He that believeth and is baptized shall be saved.'* God is intentional in providing an opportunity for all of us to serve Him. It is a privilege to be part of something that has rewards in this life and the next. When Jesus said *'Go ye into all the world'* it is not limited to a geographic region. When you are at a soccer game -that is a world. When you are on a plane -that is a world. When you are at a mall -that is a world. When you are at work -that is a world. I think you get my point. Every place we interact with is a world of opportunity to tell someone the gospel. Tell them that God loves them and He wants them to know Him through the gift of Salvation that came in the Word incarnate, Jesus Christ!

My sister and I went to a grocery store at a point we were looking for cottage cheese. While we were looking at the different flavours of cottage cheese and trying to decide, a middle-aged Indian gentleman approached us and he began a conversation about God, and linking it to the cottage cheese. We were astonished how he intertwined the topics...what started the conversation was just cottage cheese! When we were concluding, he was so bold and asked us if we were born again to make sure we get an opportunity to receive the gift of salvation. Wow, we realised, had we not been born again, we would have been led to the Lord in the grocery store! This man was fulfilling the mandate of the great commission. In another instance, when our brother started working he would commute to work by bus. The bus from Soweto to Sandton was his route. He would tell us of opportunities he'd take and just preach on the bus. He did not need a pulpit. The zeal of the gospel had consumed him (Psalms 69:9). The word of God was like fire shut up in his bones (Jeremiah 20:9). Think about it, a conversation about cottage cheese and a bus commute were opportunities to tell someone about Jesus. Telling someone about Jesus at any given opportunity is an avenue you can take in being instrumental in fulfilling the Great Commission.

The Christian journey does not end at salvation- that is only the beginning. Once one is born again, it is important to plug in to a local church. You need to be in continuous fellowship so that you grow in your journey as a Christian.

'...not neglecting to meet together, as is the habit of some, but encouraging one another...' (Hebrews 10:25)

Be part of a church community this will help identify your gifts that you can use to serve God. We all have something to contribute. We have gifts, talents and resources we can use in our local church. When Moses was instructed by God to build the tabernacle, He (God) mentioned that He had anointed craftsmen Bezalel and Oholiab who will help him with finishings.

"Bezalel and Oholiab and every craftsman in whom the Lord has put skill and intelligence to know how to do any work in the construction of the sanctuary shall work in accordance with all that the Lord has commanded." (Exodus 36:1)

Bezalel and Oholiab used their skills as craftsmen to serve God. They were skilled in all manner of craftsmanship. They were instrumental in assisting Moses to build the tabernacle according to the pattern God gave Moses. Particularly Bezalel who carved the Ark of the Covenant, his role was pivotal.

When Solomon was completing the Temple finishings, he called for Hiram to assist him in fulfilling the vision. He was skilled in crafting bronze and other metals. The splendour of the Temple was made possible by someone skilled and qualified.

'And King Solomon sent and brought Hiram from Tyre... a worker in bronze. And he was full of wisdom, understanding, and skill for making any work in bronze. He came to King Solomon and did all his work.' (1 Kings 7: 13-14)ESV

Moses and Solomon needed skilled men to accomplish the visions God gave them. You can also avail yourself in your local church. You can use your skill to the Glory of God.

Avail yourself, your ideas, your time and resources. When you serve, your input will echo into eternity.

Serving your Community

Every face has a story and behind the smiles there are nuanced layers of experiences that can be of benefit to others. You could have been raised by a teenage mom, your story can inspire young girls about the challenges ahead. You could have been a refugee and found asylum in a prosperous country, you can go back to your home country can be of encouragement. You could have been in prison for a serious crime and you are now a changed man, young men in your neighbourhood can be transformed. It could be that obtaining education was a mountain climb, now that you have conquered the precipices, you can be an inspiration to many. You could be a good sound family man loving his wife and children, you can be a prototype of a good family that someone can learn from.

The thing is, no story is insignificant. You can use your life testimony as an encouragement for others. When God wanted to set the children of Israel free and Moses came with excuses, God asked him *'What do you have in your hand?'(Exodus 4:2).*All Moses had was a rod in his hand. That same rod was instrumental for the children of Israel to see God do great exploits.

'...And thou shalt take this rod in thine hand, wherewith thou shalt do signs.' (Exodus 4:17)

After God instructed Moses, it was no longer called the rod of Moses, but the rod of God!

'...and Moses took the rod of God in his hand.' (Exodus 4:20)

In the same way God took an ordinary rod transformed it to be the rod of God. God can take your story and inspire others. God can take what you think is insignificant and use it for His glory. The question is: 'What do you have in your hand?' You might not (yet) be a multi-billionaire with a foundation, but your experiences are a starting point to inspire others. Your life story can inspire and even change someone's life. Start with what you have. See God take it and change the trajectory of your life and that of others.

The Garb of Humility

When you read the biographies of the richest people of our time, you cannot help but be inspired. It is encouraging to see how determination and hard work can enable someone to achieve so much. I came across an article of someone who had significantly achieved. They described how they grew up poor, subsequently went to school and rising to being the person they are today. A comment they made alluding to how come they were successful, they responded by saying "I am self-made." Upon reading that, I was stunned. I could not fathom how this person could not see that at every iteration of their lives, someone contributed to the person they are now.

Just think about this for a while, had they not had teachers, they wouldn't be able to read, write and communicate. Had the administrative clerk at University not processed their application, they wouldn't have the qualification. Had the taxi driver not driven them to their first job interview, they would not have access to the opportunities. At any given time, someone plays a role to contribute to your success-no matter how insignificant. There is a proverb in isi-Zulu that states *'Umunt' ungumuntu ngabantu'*. It simply means a person is a person because of others. Once you recognise that, you reflect on your personal journey and by so doing you are humbled by the contribution of others to your life, no matter how small the role.

In order to understand humility, we have to know what pride is and how God feels about pride. When you see how God detests pride, it becomes very sobering, that you will continually seek to be counted among the humble.

God resists the proud

'But He giveth more grace. Wherefore He saith, God resisteth the proud, but giveth grace unto the humble.' (James 4:6)

'And I will break the pride of your power; and I will make your heaven as iron, and your earth as brass' (Leviticus 26:19)

Pride comes with a fall

'When pride cometh, then cometh shame: but with the lowly is wisdom' (Proverbs 11:2)

'For the day of the Lord of hosts shall be upon every one that is proud and lofty, and upon every one that is lifted up; and he shall be brought low:'(Isaiah 2:12)

'Pride goeth before destruction, and an haughty spirit before a fall.' (Proverbs 16:18)

'Now I Nebuchadnezzar praise and extol and honour the King of heaven, all whose works are truth, and his ways judgment: and those that walk in pride he is able to abase.' (Daniel 4:34)

Pride is of Satan

'...lest being lifted up with pride he fall into the condemnation of the devil.' (1 Timothy 3:6)

'For all that is in the world, the lust of the flesh, and the lust of the eyes, and the pride of life, is not of the Father, but is of the world.' (1 John 2:16)

There are numerous verses that underpin how God feels about pride. Imagine how it is like to have the heavens shut, just because of pride or to be made low because you exalted yourself. It is imperative to pursue humility and to wear it as a cloak (1 Peter5:5). It is an intrinsic value that ought to be visible on you wherever you are. In order to cultivate humility, it starts with the simple things like greeting someone who does not work in your department in the elevator. How about showing respect to the lady who cleans the toilets? The lady at the till in the grocery store, try just saying "Thank you ma'am!" God does not take lightly what you do to the least of these(Matthew 25:40). Seek opportunities to practice humility, until it becomes an intrinsic value.

The word of God is also explicit on the benefits of humility.

Inherit the Kingdom of Heaven

'Whosoever therefore shall humble himself as this little child, the same is greatest in the Kingdom of heaven' (Matthew 18:4)

God lifts you up

'Humble yourselves in the sight of the Lord, and he shall lift you up' (James 4:10)

'Humble yourselves therefore under the mighty hand of God, that he may exalt you in due time'(1 Peter 5:6)

'...but honour shall uphold the humble in spirit.' (Proverbs 29:23)

God hears you

'Lord, thou hast heard the desire of the humble' (Psalms 10:17)

'If my people, which are called by my name, shall humble themselves, and pray, and seek my face, and turn from their wicked ways; then will I hear from heaven, and will forgive their sin, and will heal their land.' (2 Chronicles 7:14)

God is on the side of the humble. Be intentional by cultivating humility.

Integrity

I remember seeing a poster quote stating: *'If you had to be accused of being a Christian, would there be enough evidence to convict you?'* The only permissible evidence would be your track record and reputation. How would you fare? Can your reputation speak for you when you can't speak for yourself? The point is who you are when nobody is watching, that is integrity. Your character should be constant with who you are at the office, at the gym, at church, in traffic, with family, and even just chilling with your boys. I do understand that there is context, like when you meeting executives with your boss, it will be different to when you are chilling. The core is that your character should be consistent. You cannot be an unscrupulous business man during the week and be the same guy who teaches Sunday School. When it comes to your character, your life must not be compartmentalised.

When you cannot speak for yourself, your integrity should vouch for you. At some point someone accused a certain gentleman. The accusation was a malicious attack on this person's character. The person they were spreading this to, did not entertain the false accusations. He boldly responded *"I hear you, but I know so and so."* Only to find later it was a false accusation. His character and integrity spoke for him when he could not speak for himself. *'Because of my integrity you uphold me...' (Psalms 41:12).* Your integrity will uphold you. It will uphold you when rumours are spread about you. It will uphold you when there are false accusations against you. Work on building a good character. Let your yes be yes (James 5:12). Be reliable. Be dependable. For instance when you have an appointment with friends over the weekend, do you arrive at the time you set, or you arrive whenever? I mean, it's just your boys! A simple thing like keeping time is so nuanced and contributes to defining your integrity. It simply says when you say something, you do it and your word is dependable. You respect others and their time. On the contrary when you always arrive late and are unrepentant it also alludes subtle innuendos that you do not respect the people you need to meet, and you do not respect their time. In the event you might need leniency, people will revert to your previous conduct.

Integrity above all else is a thing of the heart. Your integrity will even govern your decision making process. The eleventh chapter of Proverbs, verse three states: *'The integrity of the upright shall guide them.'* With corruption being so rife, governments and companies are having anti-corruption clauses for employees, ethics committees, anti-corruption drives- the list is endless. Even if someone signs an anti-corruption pledge and their heart is not set on being a person of integrity, they end up violating that pledge. When God enters the heart of a man, he is able to change someone who is a liar to stand for truth.

> 'The heart is deceitful above all things, and
> desperately sick; who can understand it? "I the
> Lord search the heart and test the mind...'
> (Jeremiah 17:7)ESV

God is able to search the heart of man and change it. He searches the heart to show you the deceitful things. He then works with you to cultivate a heart that is pure. He then has something to work on with you...ultimately you are morphed into a person of integrity.

Application:

1. What good traits have you practised?

_____

_____

_____

_____

_____

_____

_____

_____

_____

_____

_____

_____

_____

_____

_____

_____

_____

_____

_____

_____

_____

_____

_____

_____

2. How have the good traits affected those in your life?

_____

_____

_____

_____

_____

_____

_____

_____

_____

_____

_____

_____

_____

_____

_____

_____

_____

_____

_____

_____

_____

_____

_____

_____

_____

_____

_____

3. What bad attitude would you like to change?

_____

_____

_____

_____

_____

_____

_____

_____

_____

_____

_____

_____

_____

_____

_____

_____

_____

_____

_____

_____

_____

_____

_____

_____

_____

_____

4. What action are you willing to take to change the bad attitude?

_____

_____

_____

_____

_____

_____

_____

_____

_____

_____

_____

_____

_____

_____

_____

_____

_____

_____

_____

_____

_____

_____

_____

_____

_____

_____

5. *'I did good tracker".*

This is a chart you can fill out for every act of kindness you do. The result can be a description how it made you feel or how the other person responded.

Date	Description Act of Kindness	To whom	Result

*…And who knows but that you have come to royal position **for such a time as this*** **
Esther 4:14 (NIV)

5

For such a time as this

Have you heard of Tertius? Or rather, have you read any books about him? He might not be recorded as a Greek Philosopher, or a famous Apostle, but his role was so important and he is mentioned in Romans 16:22: *'I Tertius, who wrote this epistle, salute you in the Lord.'* His role was so significant that the epistle of Romans was transcribed by him. He was an amanuensis, who was very skilled in the transcription of dictation. He was instrumental to Paul and wrote as Paul received and dictated the powerful revelation. Without him being available to assist Paul, we would not have the book of Romans. Think of where God has positioned you, like Tertius your role may seem small, but allow God to use you to find your place in history.

When a rainbow appears it is as a result of light bending when it moves through light. Water droplets refract the sun's light and this is an occurrence that happens at a moment in time. Think of your life as a moment in time and how your existence could be something for those around to marvel at. Taking up a moment of significance can be regarded as a *kairos* moment. Kairos is a Greek word for a moment in time. For a moment in time, allow His glory to shine on your life, like sunlight on a water droplet, your life will reflect the ultimate destiny He has for you. Allow Him to work through you, like the rainbow which is a sign of covenant, His plan for your life is fulfilled.

God has a plan for your life. *'For I know the plans I have for you, declares the Lord, plans for welfare and not for evil, to give you a future and a hope.' (Jeremiah 29:11, ESV).* Your role can be like that of Joseph, who was sold to slavery by his brothers and went to Egypt. He moved from the pit to the palace, from the palace to the prison from the prison to serve with Pharaoh. The ultimate plan was that the nation of Israel be born in Egypt and for God to deliver them. God had the whole nation of Israel in mind when Joseph was going through his trials (Psalms 105: 16-23). God has you in mind too. Look at the circumstances in your life, they could very well be unfolding God's plan you. Everything you go through will work out as the plan God has for your life. Position yourself so that God can orchestrate your life for His glory. You can be called in politics, sports, business or any career, just allow God to use your life for His glory.

Politics and Government

In the year 2000 there were devastating floods in Mozambique. As the water levels rose, a highly pregnant woman climbed up a tree in an effort to save herself and the life of her unborn baby. The South African National Defence Force (SANDF) conducted a rescue operation. In the nick of time, they rescued this woman on the top of the tree. She was in labour. They helped deliver her baby right there on the top of the tree. This was a miracle baby indeed. Television cameras and reporters were covering this story. After being brought to safety, in one of the interviews the mother was asked, what she hopes the baby will be in future. She responded: *"I'd like her to be a (government) minister or a big leader."* I marvelled at the choice in career. I thought to myself, probably the way to success is having a position in government. Perhaps being a government official carries prestige.

With that said, what if God has called you to lead in the political arena? You might not be about status and privilege, but you really want to serve. When you look at the way things are being administrated, there is a burden in your heart. You might feel frustrated when you hear reports on corruption. You see a better way on how the education system can be improved. You see a better way on how hospitals can have advanced better health care. You see a better way on how the economy can be revitalised. Maybe like Moses, you are burdened by the status quo in your country.

'And it came to pass in those days, when Moses was grown, that he went unto his bretheren, and looked on their burdens' (Exodus 2:11)

In seeing the burdens of his fellow Hebrews he was compelled to act. He was so passionate about their plight that he ended up killing an Egyptian who was ill-treating a Hebrew (Exodus2: 11-12). Little did he know, someone saw him and reminded him of it. This caused Moses to flee and be exiled in Midian. That passion and zeal to see the Israelites free did not leave him. After forty years on the run, he had the burning bush experience that made him return to Egypt. He had to go back to Pharaoh demanding freedom for the Hebrews. A stutterer boldly declaring God's message *'Let My people go!'* A burden never leaves you. When you have a burden it is beyond writing a comment on social media. It goes beyond being part of a protest once off. It is that thing in your heart that does not let go. You do not get satisfied with the status quo, you get compelled to do something about it. God can use that burden in your heart to change the trajectory of a generation. You could be so instrumental and influential that it could be said of you like David, that you served your generation. *'For David after he had served his own generation by the will of God ...' (Acts 13:36).*

When you read about David, you realise that he had to make a lot of conquests for Israel. His historical moment came when he defeated Goliath (1 Samuel 17). That was a career propelling move. He was thrust from being a shepherd to being king shortly after Saul lost favour with God. He served his generation with the multiple conquests and establishing Israel (2 Samuel 5:20). He served his generation by returning the Ark of the Lord to Israel from the Philistines (2 Samuel 6). Once his tenure ended his son

Solomon reigned in his stead. Solomon had to build the temple after David died without having done so.'...*David my father could not build a house unto the name of the Lord his God for the wars which were about him on every side...'(1 Kings 5:3).*

David fought wars and Solomon had to build the temple. David was purposeful such that Solomon as the next generation, did not have to deal with wars that he (David) had to fight. Each generation has a purpose and it must be identified. For example on the continent of Africa, most countries received independence in the 1950s and 60s. That era of fighting for independence can be compared to David's era of fighting wars. The era of building, like that of Solomon, follows after wars. When Solomon was king over Israel, there was peace and prosperity. The era of building brings with it peace and prosperity.

'And Judah and Israel dwelt safely, everyman under his vine and under his fig tree, from Dan even to Beersheba, all the days of Solomon'(1 Kings 4:25)

Solomon being the wisest man to have lived ensured to continue from the legacy that David left behind, he built! He built such that the prosperity that was experienced in building the temple cascaded throughout the kingdom. The prosperity was such that people across the kingdom had vines and figs. Figs and vines are symbolic for abundance, peace and security. Each generation was served respectively by David and Solomon. How are you serving yours?

You could ask yourself…How can I serve my generation? There could be a burden in your heart looking at the political status quo. Allow God to channel your passion so that you can find an opportunity to serve your generation. Maybe your era is to have conquests like David…or maybe to build like Solomon. Whatever it is, may God steer you in the direction of your calling… Lord knows, you could be your country's next '*Mr. President*!'

Business and Career

You could be hustling and having the *Empire State of Mind*… Or for you it's all about the *Benjamins*? Or you work to earn money, power and respect…Or when it comes to money you could be the hero, writing them cheques with a whole lot of zeros…it's the God in you!

In case you missed it, we are talking about money! Should Christian men have (lots of) money? Should Christian men occupy positions of power and influence? These questions challenge the status quo and remove the stereotype that Christians should not be in the market place. Tradition has influenced that Christians should live up to the old saying *as poor as a church mouse*. Moreover, that Christians be in churches and keep away from the main stream. In the parable when Jesus speaks of the nobleman who went to a far country, gave his servants ten minas and left them with the words '*Engage in business until I come*' (Luke 19:7) *ESV*. We can take heed of this instruction. We ought to go to the market place, engage in business, build careers, in sports, the arts…*occupy 'till He come*!

You can do this being a born again, God loving, Holy Spirit filled and anointed child of God. Being born again connects you to the Abrahamic blessing (Galatians 3:13-14). Being filled by the Holy Spirit enables you to take heed as He imparts wisdom and gives you direction and ideas (John 16:13). The anointing empowers you and teaches you all things(1 John 2:27) The purpose of excelling in business and your career is to give glory to God and to see that the Kingdom of God comes on earth as it is in heaven (Matthew 6:10). When the primary goal is to glorify God, it defines the purpose for initiating a career or business initiative. It is also a fulfilment of what God said in the beginning that we be fruitful and multiply (Genesis 1:28). Moreover, when Moses was giving the children of Israel the law, he emphasised that God gives the ability to get wealth, such that He establishes His covenant with them.

'But thou shalt remember the Lord thy God: for it is he that giveth thee power to get wealth, that he may establish his covenant which he sware unto thy fathers, as it is this day' (Deuteronomy 8:18)

The higher life for a Christian is not only to be blessed. The higher life is to be blessed to be a blessing (Genesis 22:17). It is a given that money is a subsequent result of prosperity in your business and career. Money takes on the character of who is handling it. If money is in the hands of a child of God, it will result in ministry initiatives being financed as well as advancing the Kingdom of God. There are several examples of people who were in positions of influence and were affluent, who advanced God's work with their position and affluence:

Joseph

'And Pharaoh said unto Joseph, See, I have set thee over all the land of Egypt...And he made him to ride in the second chariot which he had; and they cried before him, Bow the knee: and he made him ruler over all the land of Egypt' *(Genesis 41:41,43)*

Daniel

'Then the king gave Daniel high honors and many great gifts, and made him ruler over the whole province of Babylon and chief prefect over all the wise men of Babylon.' *(Daniel 2:48)*

Shunammite Woman

'One day Elisha went on to Shunem, where a wealthy woman lived, who urged him to eat some food' *(2 Kings 4:8)ESV*

Job

'His substance also was seven thousand sheep, and three thousand camels, and five hundred yoke of oxen, and five hundred she asses, and a very great household; so that this man was the greatest of all the men of the east.' *(Job 1:3)*

Lydia

'...And a certain woman named Lydia, a seller of purple, of the city of Thyatira, which worshipped God, heard us: whose heart the Lord opened, that she attended unto the things which were spoken of Paul.' (Acts 16:14)

As you see, children of God have occupied positions of influence and have been wealthy. Find your place in the market place- get in the system. You can start by being a street vendor, have an online store, run a small business or even own a conglomerate- find a place to occupy. You can start your role as junior, rise to middle management, then you are at the helm in the corner office- just occupy. When we have children of God in the market place, God establishes His covenant with them and they advance the Kingdom. May the Kingdom come on earth as it is in heaven!

In Prison

You could be in prison reading this book. You might think to yourself *'Of what good can I be, when I am locked up.'* God has you in mind too. Someone said that from his time in prison Genesis 28:16 resonated well with him. It states: *'...Surely the Lord is in this place and I knew it not.'* He said while others were tormented by nightmares and lived in regret of their actions, he found solace and peace in God. God can be found in the most obscure of places. Even in circumstances that seem to be the worst, God still makes

Himself known to all men. Even from behind bars God can reach you, and your life can have impact.

Some people are in prison for crimes they did not commit. Unfortunately miscarriages of justice do occur. A case in point is a young man I read about, who was released from prison after serving 18 years. He was sentenced to life in prison for murder. After several failed appeals at lower courts, a High Court ruled that it was mistaken identity, and he was released. He was nineteen years old when he started serving the time and got released at the age of 37.

Maybe your story is unlike that of the aforementioned man and you are serving the time for what you did. How can God give your life have meaning beyond this? God promises that He will not condemn you. *'There is therefore now no condemnation to them which are in Christ Jesus, who walk not after the flesh, but after the Spirit' (Romans 8:1).* God will provide freedom from within that you do not live in condemnation. Once you don't live in condemnation, and pursue the things of the Spirit, He starts a work in you when you decide to surrender all to Him. You can start by asking forgiveness from God, forgiveness from those you hurt and finally forgive yourself. It becomes a journey. The journey starts when you decide to be transformed by the word of God.

> *'And be not conformed to this world, but be ye transformed by the renewing of your mind that ye may prove what is that good and acceptable. And perfect will of God' (Romans 12:2)*

1. Do not conform to <u>this</u> world

I think you can agree with me when I say prison is a world on its own. There are gangs, smugglers of weapons, money, drugs, alcohol etc. Once you are in prison you have to find survival mechanisms just to make it through the day, let alone the duration of your sentence. With that said, the word of God says *'Do not conform'*. Not conforming means not aligning to the standard of where you are. Know who you are in Christ such that you don't become the environment you are in. Remember that the decisions you make daily will outlive you and be a seed for the family on the outside. Be intentional in planting good seed as your lineage will reap the fruit of the seed of your actions. Rise above your surroundings and environment… *do not conform!*

2. Be transformed by the renewing of your mind

Only God can change a man! God is able to change a man such that everything about his character is a shadow of his former self. Can you imagine changing right before your own eyes and that of others. The thing is, God does the saving, but you are a critical component for the transformation. You are held responsible for the transformation roadmap and ensuring you renew your mind. Daily you can have the word of God until your mind is renewed, and then you are ultimately transformed. It is a journey, take it and you will see the change. While on the journey, you can even say about yourself: *'I may not be where I want to be, but surely I am not where I used to be!'* Allow God to work in you…be ye transformed.

3. Being In God's Will

The journey with God continually unfolds. He intends for us to live out His perfect will. Three levels of God's will are listed the good, acceptable and the perfect will. The good is that you are a child of God, through the gift of salvation. The second is the acceptable will. The acceptable will can be likened to compromising God's word when faced with difficult choices. Then there is the perfect will of God. This is the place where you experience God's best, in accordance to His promises as a result of your obedience. Don't settle just for good, or acceptable. Pursue God's perfect will…even from behind bars.

I read about Charles Colson who was the legal advisor for US President Nixon during the Watergate Scandal. He went to serve time for his role. After he was released, he started Prison Fellowship International, a ministry that impacts prisons around the world, operating in more than 120 countries. Similarly, may God's word transform you that even from your circumstance your life will impact others and ultimately being glory to Him.

Wherever you may find yourself, align to God's will and you will be able to fulfil your destiny.

Application:

1. What issues are affecting your community or
   country?

   _____

   _____

   _____

   _____

   _____

   _____

   _____

   _____

   _____

   _____

   _____

   _____

   _____

   _____

   _____

   _____

   _____

   _____

   _____

   _____

   _____

   _____

   _____

   _____

   _____

2. How do you see yourself getting involved in solving the issues in your community or country?

_____

_____

_____

_____

_____

_____

_____

_____

_____

_____

_____

_____

_____

_____

_____

_____

_____

_____

_____

_____

_____

_____

_____

_____

_____

_____

_____

3. What are your goals (short-term, mid-term, long term)?

_____

_____

_____

_____

_____

_____

_____

_____

_____

_____

_____

_____

_____

_____

_____

_____

_____

_____

_____

_____

_____

_____

_____

_____

_____

_____

_____

_____

4. Develop a plan to achieving your goals.

_____

_____

_____

_____

_____

_____

_____

_____

_____

_____

_____

_____

_____

_____

_____

_____

_____

_____

_____

_____

_____

_____

_____

_____

_____

_____

_____

_____

_____

_____

5. What is your picture of success?

_____

_____

_____

_____

_____

_____

_____

_____

_____

_____

_____

_____

_____

_____

_____

_____

_____

_____

_____

_____

_____

_____

_____

_____

_____

_____

_____

_____

_____

6. How do you see yourself impacting your generation?

_____

_____

_____

_____

_____

_____

_____

_____

_____

_____

_____

_____

_____

_____

_____

_____

_____

_____

_____

_____

_____

_____

_____

_____

_____

'*...I washed my steps with butter, and the rock poured me out rivers of oil*'
Job 29:6

6

Becoming the Job 29 Man

Who is the Job 29 Man? What is so intriguing about him that the pinnacle point of this book is based on him? Theologians the world over have made studies and commentaries about the book of Job. When reading the first chapter, it gives insight on the type of man Job was. He was a man blameless and upright, one who feared God and turned away from evil (Job 1:1,8). However even though he was faithful to God, Satan attacked him. Job lost everything he had. His wealth, his children his prestige and his wife! In Job 29, Job reminisces on the man he was before experienced the tumultuous season. He is not lamenting, but reflecting on the man he knew himself to have been. What I like about Job 29, it epitomises the man who is described as blameless and upright. It is a man who walks with God, a man who commands authority, a man who cares and generously provides for others and a man who leads in humility.

A Man Who Walks With God

'Job now resumed his response: "Oh, how I long for the good old days, when God took such very good care of me. He always held a lamp before me and I walked through the dark by its light. Oh, how I miss those golden years when God's friendship graced my home, When the Mighty One was still by my side and my children were all around me, When everything was going my way, and nothing seemed too difficult.' (Job 29:1-6) MSG

Job loved God. In him loving God, it was as if the Lord's face shone upon him (Numbers 6:24-25). God made his paths lit and prosperous. God would be manifest in his family affairs as his children would be around him. These are the results of a man walking with God. It becomes seen that your life is under His covering. In verse six it states *'I washed my steps with butter, and the rock poured me out rivers of oil'*. Butter and oil in this context refer to cream, or lushness, or abundance. A man who walks with God experiences God's providence. God opulently blesses a man who walks with Him...this ultimately gives glory back to God! Even in our time we need to see men who unequivocally follow God and we see them prosper in our mist. God intends to fulfil His word to every generation. Yield yourself to God and His way of doing things and see yourself inherit God's blessing.

A Man Who Commands Authority

'When I walked downtown and sat with my friends in the public square, Young and old greeted me with respect; I was honoured by everyone in town. When I spoke, everyone listened; they hung on my every word. People who knew me spoke well of me; my reputation went ahead of me.'(Job 29:7-10)MSG

In the East in Job's era the public square and the gate were places of authority. The people who would sit at the gate would be elders and they would ensure what is discussed at the gate would be a rule for the city. If Job was permitted to stand and speak at the gate, it meant he exerted a certain level of authority. He was honoured and respected by the young and the old. His authority was well-founded as when he spoke people listened.

There will be opportunities granted to you where you can exercise your authority. Grab a hold of them and take a chance to lead. This means your reputation and humility should go before you such that coercive power is not displayed. It is an authority that operates with grace, undergirded by dignity. When the opportunity presents itself, be ready and like Job, you will be honoured.

A Man Who Cares And Generously Provides For Others

'When the ear heard me, then it blessed me; and when the eye saw me, it gave witness to me: Because I delivered the

poor that cried, and the fatherless, and him that had none to help him. The blessing of him that was ready to perish came upon me: and I caused the widow's heart to sing for joy. I put on righteousness, and it clothed me: my judgment was as a robe and a diadem. I was eyes to the blind, and feet was I to the lame. I was a father to the poor: and the cause which I knew not I searched out. And I brake the jaws of the wicked, and plucked the spoil out of his teeth. Then I said, I shall die in my nest, and I shall multiply my days as the sand. My root was spread out by the waters, and the dew lay all night upon my branch. My glory was fresh in me, and my bow was renewed in my hand.' (Job 29:11-20)MSG

Job was a man who took care of the needs of others. The wealth he was emancipated with, he used it to be a blessing to others. The orphans, widows, those who mourn were all taken care of in Job's presence. When God blesses you, He wants you to give glory back to Him by ensuring that you become His hands and feet. You are blessed to be a blessing. Job's generosity was evident to those around him, as they rejoiced in his presence. He also was a man who would seek justice for the poor. Who are you known as? What does your reputation say about you? What is the plight of the poor in your community? If you have it within your means to support those less fortunate than you and extend a helping hand.

A man who leads in Humility

"Men and women listened when I spoke, hung expectantly on my every word. After I spoke, they'd be quiet, taking it

all in. They welcomed my counsel like spring rain, drinking it all in. When I smiled at them, they could hardly believe it; their faces lit up, their troubles took wing! I was their leader, establishing the mood and setting the pace by which they lived. Where I led, they followed." (Job 29: 21-25) MSG

Job provided godly and wise counsel. The people he led would be attentive to him and give him the honour and respect due to him. He could have that reciprocated to him because that is what he gave out. He was humble and that created an atmosphere where people submitted to his leadership. A man with seven thousand sheep, and three thousand camels, and five hundred yoke of oxen, and five hundred she asses, and a very great household also greatest of all the men of the east, definitely had people administrating his wealth. Yet, his wealth and riches did not define him. Instead, he was humble and those around him revered him.

Lessons from Job 29

Job lived blamelessly and he feared God. The testimony of his life at his prime is indicative of a man who many can look up to in terms of developing good characteristics. Job was one man and his impact transcended from his family, to his community to the entire region of the East (Job 1:3).

When God wants to do something spectacular, he singles people out. Job was one man who through his faithfulness was chosen by God to show the value of being a man who obeys God's laws. He received wealth, a good family and respect from people and was highly regarded by God (Job 1: 1-5). God does not operate with a crowd. He will either use one man, or a few who prove themselves faithful. He just needs a remnant from a generation. There are other examples that we can refer to whereby God chooses one person or a few.

Abraham

Father Abraham was one man and all the nations of the earth are blessed through him.

'And I will make of thee a great nation, and I will bless thee, and make thy name great; and thou shalt be a blessing: And I will bless them that bless thee, and curse him that curseth thee: and in thee shall all families of the earth be blessed.' (Genesis 12:2-3)

Jesus

Jesus chose twelve disciples to start His ministry. Their impact was world-wide.

'And Jesus going up to Jerusalem took the twelve disciples apart in the way, and said unto them' (Matthew 20:17)

Gideon

Gideon needed 300 men to defeat the army of the Midianites.

'And the Lord said unto Gideon, By the three hundred men that lapped will I save you, and deliver the Midianites into thine hand: and let all the other people go every man unto his place' (Judges 7:7)

The journey to being the man God has created you to be starts with you making a choice to be chosen when you obey and follow His statutes. You make a choice on being moulded by God and be counted among the remnant.

May it be you will be stirred up to be counted as a remnant that will impact your family, community, country and generation. May it be said of you that like David, you served your generation. May it be said of you that you cracked the code and in your generation you were counted among the *gentle*men...You were the Job 29 Man!

My Job 29 Man Pledge #IAMJOB29

I _____ pledge to myself and God that from this day forward I commit to the following:

1. I will be a man who seeks the First the Kingdom, seeks the Lord and His Word.

2. I will continue the legacy of faith I have inherited from my predecessors/ I will be a new seed and establish a new altars for my lineage.

3. I will present my body as a living sacrifice, holy and acceptable unto the Lord.

4. I will be a man who operates in kindness, servitude, humility and integrity.

5. I will seek my destiny, fulfil my purpose and serve my generation.

Signed _____

Date _____

Notes

i   Szalay Jessie, *'Marco Polo: Facts, Biography Travels'*, LiveScience, 27 February 2013 https://www.livescience.com/27513-marco-polo.html

ii Christian Examiner, *'700-year-old-gospel-challenge-in-mongolia-is-answered'*, Christian Examiner, 17 January 2009, http://www.christianexaminer.com/article/700-year-old-gospel-challenge-in-mongolia-is-answered/43038.htm

iii Munroe Myles, *Rediscovering the Kingdom*, Bahamas: Destiny Image Publishers Inc,2004, (p64-66)

iv Stone Perry, *'Purging your home and pruning your family tree'*, Charisma House,2014, (p 82)

v   Nwaka Benard. *'The Mystery of the altar'*. Grace Bible Church, Pimville, Soweto. 28 March 2010. Sermon

vi Heward-Mills Dag, *'Formula for Humility'*, Parchment House, 2013 (2016)